More Than 90 Minutes

ALEJANDRO PÉREZ

MORE THAN 90 MINUTES

ANALYZING SUCCESS IN EUROPEAN CLUB SOCCER

Meyer & Meyer Sport

British Library Cataloguing in Publication Data

A catalogue record for this book is available from the British Library

More Than 90 Minutes

Maidenhead: Meyer & Meyer Sport (UK) Ltd., 2017

ISBN: 978-1-78255-122-5

Aachen, Auckland, Beirut, Cairo, Cape Town, Dubai, Hägendorf, Hong Kong, Indianapolis, Manila, New Delhi, Singapore, Sydney, Tehran, Vienna

Member of the World Sports Publishers' Association (WSPA)

Printed by: C-M Books, Ann Arbor, MI, USA

ISBN: 978-1-78255-122-5

Email: info@m-m-sports.com

www.m-m-sports.com

CONTENTS

PREFACE

When football entered my life, it didn't leave space for much else. Even though it didn't take away, nor ever will, my passion for films, music, and a glass of wine, it became the center of my life, including my very ambitious professional goals.

Getting up every very early Saturdays and Sundays to watch marathons of matches, staying up late during Champions League matchdays to watch three matches, and doing what it takes to watch an important match is a routine that I have kept in the last fifteen years of my life and perhaps will never change.

One night in 2008, I decided it was time to start writing some ideas and concepts I had already been forming in my mind; they had started to pile up, and I was worried they might never become a reality. In the blank sheets of Lilien's, my partner at the time, school notebook, I wrote out these ideas and began fitting the pieces of a puzzle I ended up completing nine years later after watching thousands of matches and taking notes and making analyses that sometimes prevented me from sleeping.

More Than 90 Minutes has truly been a journey of discovery, improvement, and even joy. Although I sometimes leaned my head against the wall when I couldn't shape an idea, or I actually wondered if someone would ever be interested in reading what, in my opinion, was a compelling text, I always found a way over the bumps in the road—the rejection every writer experiences with his own manuscript. Sometimes I celebrated as if I had scored a fantastic goal. This book represents the finished product of my journey. Enjoy.

ACKNOWLEDGMENTS

Though I am the sole author of this book, getting the energy and focus to finish this book would have been almost impossible without some monumental people who gave me the motivation to set my sights on my goals and the perseverance needed to achieve them.

To my mother and my father for that unconditional and natural guidance. Now I can confidently highlight it as one of the pillars of my life.

To Lilien for being with me in a very prolific stage of my life and for standing so many "I can't go with you to visit your family because there are so many matches I have to watch" and for constantly affirming that you only need to wish something to make that dream come true.

To Albe for his immeasurable humility and for letting me watch so many matches, like Maday, Guerman, Rafa, and the Ameijeiras' guys did.

And most importantly, even though silently and without being able to understand the magnitude of her masterpiece, to Muñi, for making me a better person and for showing the path to dedication and perseverance and how focused we should be when we want to achieve the things that really matter in life, the ones you get after so many years of hard work and keeping your sight relentlessly on the place you want to be.

INTRODUCTION

Football is not an exact science. On many occasions 2+2 does not make four. Nobody is the holder of absolute truth, and it is impossible to find a player, a manager, or a team that has never had to go through a hard time.

In football, you never stop learning. Its wealth is such that in order to continue to be a successful professional, whether on the pitch or on the bench, evolution is a compulsory process. No team, formula, or system has lasted over time and been immune to the cunning of rivals or the decadence which is implicit in any process.

Indeed, that makes it even richer, as there is an infinite number of ways to reach success, just as there is an infinite number of ways to achieve failure. Being coherent, consistent, daring, astute, mentally strong, humble, indefatigable, and brave are the basic ingredients to achieve a long and fruitful career in this art. Only those who are great know how to mix them and make the magic cocktail.

Special note on the text: Throughout the book, the British term, "football," is used.

Chapter 1

ATTACKERS WHO DEFEND AND DEFENDERS WHO ATTACK—TWO VERY DIFFERENT THINGS

Toward the end of his first spell at Chelsea, José Mourinho had produced a side that had gradually become more solid and more compact. This was due in no small part to the arrival of men who helped make his tactical provisions a reality. With Michael Essien and Michael Ballack in the midfield and Didier Drogba as center forward, Mourinho changed his ideas to the point where he played with just one forward, which didn't go too badly for him because the Ivory Coast striker was able to cope all on his own leading the line.

Signing Andriy Shevchenko seemed to mean Mourinho would be compelled to play with two up front, but the poor form the Ukrainian was in made him stick to 4–4–1–1, with Joe Cole fulfilling a mixed role, although largely with midfield responsibilities.

The great goal-scoring threat of Frank Lampard, not to mention that of Ballack, contributed greatly to the success of that system, as the solidity of the midfield and the colossal defense starring John

Terry, Ricardo Carvalho, and Petr Cech meant that Chelsea often only needed one goal to win all three points.

Indeed, it was the arrival of Essien, and subsequently of Ballack, that threatened to undermine Lampard's great box-to-box prowess.

In the 2003-2004 season, when Chelsea reached the Champions League semi-final, winning at Highbury against the Arsenal Invincibles, Lampard had one of the best seasons of any player that decade.

At that time, the manager was Claudio Ranieri. He allowed Lampard to cover an enormous amount of ground to both recover and distribute the ball, which was key to his fantastic play that year. Ranieri's Chelsea had a phenomenal season and missed out on winning the league because Arsène Wenger's Invincibles played football from another planet and were just that—invincible.

Lampard needed that huge area to express himself fully on the pitch. It may seem illogical, but with a smaller area to play in, he would lose some of his impact.

The arrival of Mourinho—who didn't have an intimate knowledge of the inner workings of Ranieri's Chelsea—and the Abramovich signings, Essien among them, restricted Lampard's space; he began to lose his place in the midfield and had to start to adapt in order to continue to play a key role.

In several Champions League games in the 2006–2007 season, Mourinho played Makelele, Lampard, Ballack, Essien, Drogba, and Shevchenko. A team that was impossible to get through, but with a midfield so heavily populated with players with similar characteristics that the speed down the wings offered by Arjen Robben and Shaun Wright-Phillips wasn't exploited. This had the effect of diminishing the usefulness of a player like Lampard, as he played his best football when he had a lot of space around him.

That transformation in Chelsea's style of play impacted negatively on their own performances because with a less densely populated midfield they won two consecutive league titles, but then they declined sharply. It wasn't until Carlo Ancelotti's arrival that they became champions of England again.

A perfect example of how it's possible to defend with attackers and do it well is the Manchester United-Chelsea game played on January 11, 2009, when Luiz Felipe Scolari hadn't yet been replaced with Guus Hiddink. On that occasion at Old Trafford, Scolari played John Obi Mikel, Lampard, Ballack, and Deco in midfield, while Ferguson just gave Darren Fletcher the more defensive duties, with Ryan Giggs next to him, Ronaldo and Park Ji-sung on the wings, and Wayne Rooney and Dimitar Berbatov up front. Result: Manchester United barely broke a sweat all afternoon, created endless opportunities, and ran out convincing 3-0 winners, marking the start of their final push to displace Chelsea and Liverpool at the top of the league and win their third title in a row.

A few months later in Milan, a similar tactical revolution took place that achieved even greater results. The man behind it, surprisingly enough, was none other than Mourinho himself; the same Mourinho who at Chelsea had decided to increase the number of midfielders and build a football team based on fewer natural attackers had now decided to try a completely different tack.

At the start of the 2009-2010 season—his second at the San Siro—Mourinho used Samuel Eto'o as a lone striker against Dynamo Kiev in the group stage of the Champions League, which suggested a return to his old Chelsea ways. Fortunately for Inter and for world football, that match ended in a 2-2 draw, and Mourinho realized that formation wouldn't take him where he wanted to go.

The presence of one of the best forwards in the world such as Eto'o and the tremendous form Diego Milito was in forced Mourinho to be more conventional and put them both up front. When he saw the number of goals that strike pair produced, he kept them as his main offensive weapon, although we may wonder just how carefully he had to consider it.

But the biggest change in Mourinho's mentality came in the Champions League last sixteen match against Chelsea. If at the same point the previous year against Manchester United he wanted to play chess rather than football and clung to an overly cautious formation, now Mourinho started the first leg with Eto'o, Milito, and another of the new ever-presents, Wesley Sneijder. He surprised half the watching world and showed that you can learn from your knocks and knockouts.

After just three minutes, Inter was up 1-0; they kept attacking Chelsea and after half-time, with Inter ahead 2-1, he realized that that score line left them vulnerable for the return leg at Stamford Bridge, so after thirteen minutes of the second half he replaced Thiago Motta with Mario Balotelli. In other words, he ended up playing with Sneijder and three forwards.

Although the score didn't change, that doesn't detract from the excellent football displayed by Inter or, in particular, the evolution in thinking of the hereto quite rigid Mourinho.

In the return leg in London, he continued with his revolutionary formation and started with Sneijder, Goran Pandev, Milito, and Eto'o. He came out with all guns blazing, forcing Chelsea to go in search of goals but at the same time take great care in defense, things that can't always be successfully combined. That game showed how football is sometimes like a small blanket; if you cover your feet, your head sticks out, and vice versa.

The pressure on the Chelsea back line was so great that they found it difficult to attack in sufficient numbers to penetrate a very solid Inter defense led by an excellent Lúcio. The game was very even with two well-matched teams. Mourinho knew he was playing against a great team and that there was a real chance of being knocked out, but the best way to leave Stamford Bridge alive was to attack without fear.

And that's what they did. They attacked their opponent and avoided being attacked. They didn't concede, and when Carlo Ancelotti decided he needed to make a couple of changes, which weakened his defense, Eto'o scored to decide the tie.

Bad luck for Chelsea; they got a hard draw against a team who played even harder and who lost the tag of European lightweights. Mourinho took Inter Milan to the quarter-final with a masterful display of football, just as Guus Hiddink's Chelsea had done a year before against Liverpool.

The games against CSKA in the quarter-final allowed him a breather before facing what was to come in the semi-final: Barcelona. Here he produced another shock and qualified for the final and a trophy for which Inter had been yearning since 1965.

In the first leg, played at home, Mourinho kept his ultra-attacking formation and got a scarcely imaginable 3-1 victory, giving him a huge cushion for the return leg. Not many teams in the previous two seasons had managed to win by that score against a Barça who the previous year had won the treble, much less come back from a goal down to do so. In the return leg, Mourinho was about to employ the same starting eleven, but Pandev got injured during the warm-up, so Mourinho decided to use Christian Chivu as left back and move Javier Zanetti into a three-man midfield alongside Thiago Motta and Esteban Cambiasso. He could afford the luxury of doing this because it didn't suit him to go toe to toe with a Barcelona side who would be going all out for the two goals they needed to reach the final.

After twenty-eight minutes, the game changed dramatically with the unfair dismissal of Motta, and Inter had no choice but to batten down the hatches in their own area to weather the storm.

And they managed it. Barça's only goal came in the eighty-third minute, and although Bojan Krkić had two golden opportunities to decide the tie—one missed header and another which was disallowed for offside—that second goal never arrived.

When the final whistle went, Mourinho ran toward the pitch and stood before the Camp Nou in one of the most defiant poses ever seen on a football pitch, which was understandable to a point because of the ridiculous red card shown to one of his best players.

In the final, they played a Bayern Munich side who, without being solid or having a clear identity, had done enough to get through the three knockout rounds, though the first two not without a fight. Arjen Robben saved their skins against Fiorentina and Manchester United, and then in the semi-final they came up against an Olympique Lyonnais side who had little to offer for an occasion of that magnitude.

The first Champions League final to be held on a Saturday was a little strange because Inter hadn't been in one since 1972, and Bayern's continental reputation had suffered a little, despite having eliminated Manchester United on the way to the final.

While the German team had a very tricky group with Bordeaux and Juventus, and they needed an epic victory in Turin in the last game, in the three knockout rounds they came up against two sides outside the top tier of European football—Fiorentina and Lyon. Quite the opposite was true of Inter, who had to get past two of the favorites to win the competition in the shape of Chelsea and Barça.

The final on May 22 at the Santiago Bernabéu had the additional spice of being a meeting of two old acquaintances from the Camp Nou: the astute Mourinho, who could deal with the abrupt van Gaal and take advantage of his four years in Barcelona, including the season spent there with Bobby Robson.

Despite having gotten through round after round, Bayern showed that they lacked the firepower necessary to go head to head with a tough and well-oiled team such as Inter, who again took to the field with Sneijder and three forwards.

The tremendous goal-scoring form of Diego Milito, who had enjoyed one of the best seasons of any forward in recent years, was an unstoppable weapon against Bayern, who relied on the mobility of Ivica Olić or the genius of Robben, as Ribéry had been foolishly sent off by Roberto Rosetti against Lyon and was ineligible for the final.

What was to become Mourinho's star lineup in the second half of the season has certain points that stand out for analysis. The most surprising and praiseworthy is that, for the first time in his life, he put three forwards and a number 10 on the field, although in practice Eto'o and Pandev weren't exactly forwards positionally speaking, but rather hard-working midfielders more focused on marking and bringing the ball forward, and not so much on scoring, as the responsibility for that lay mainly with Diego Milito.

Eto'o and Pandev might point to those four months as the time when they ran most in their lives, but Mourinho's brilliant tactic of defending with attackers ended up bringing him no less than the treble.

The wit both forwards showed in adapting to their new functions, integrating in the defensive transitions and retaining their offensive threat when the team won the ball back, was a Mourinho masterstroke which, funnily enough, may have stemmed from a "let's suck it and see" approach, since it had nothing whatever in common with the product he ended up building in his last months at Chelsea.

This doesn't mean that it's a model that should be implemented across the board and that anyone who does will end up winning a treble. The success of a football team depends on many factors, but in this case, everything came together: the manager's daring, his footballers' flexibility, superb understanding on the pitch, and, as always, the thing which is never missing, luck.

The fact that Inter were concentrating a little more on the Champions League meant they had an unexpected blip in Serie A and temporarily lost the lead to Roma. That stuttering run-in was affected—greatly—by rotation, particularly in defense, where Inter were much more vulnerable when they didn't play with their two first-choice center backs, Lúcio and Walter Samuel.

The defeat to Catania was the low point of Inter's collapse in Serie A, where Marco Materazzi made a real fool of himself by chasing Malaca Martínez all around the area like a ten-year-old boy before watching him score into an empty net.

But they had the luck of champions; Giampaolo Pazzini and Sampdoria gave them a hand by beating Roma in the Stadio Olimpico to give them the title. Roma, managed by Ranieri, lacked the solidity a serious title contender needs. A home game—true, against a good team in Sampdoria—with a Roman storm raining down on Storari's goal but which ended with two goals by Pazzini which Roma, with Totti now on the pitch, had no answer to it.

Inter's magical year was completed by winning the Coppa Italia in a final Roma might have seen as a chance to make up a little for having allowed the league to escape from their clutches. However, they offered a performance that wasn't worthy of the quality of players they had, starting with their ineffectiveness as a goal-scoring threat and finishing with the deplorable attitude of Francesco Totti and his kick out at Mario Balotelli.

CHOLO'S STORY

El Cholo Simeone once said that the second half of a season is usually more difficult for teams fighting for the league title because many of their opponents are more focused on getting a point than on playing.

Without losing their exuberant desire to win every game and perhaps without meaning to, Atlético de Madrid was gradually consumed in Simeone's existential endeavor in the final months of the 2013-2014 season, the season that not only brought them the Spanish league title, but also snatched the Champions League victory away from them even as they seemed about to savor its sweet taste. Their goal-scoring threat was diminishing all the time, and their center backs became the side's biggest weapon, both in their own area and in the opposition's.

Once Diego Costa started to miss games repeatedly because of injury, Simeone adopted an approach fairly similar to that of Mourinho in the first season of his second spell at Chelsea: defend better in order to try and win 1-0. Fairly similar, but not identical.

The Argentine manager didn't have too much confidence in his other forwards replacing his first-choice center forward and decided to rely on the aerial threat offered by Miranda and Diego Godín from set pieces. Indeed, on several occasions, when Atlético were drawing matches, he took off one of his attackers and put on José Ernesto Sosa to gain more precision when it came to set pieces.

Atlético de Madrid scored three goals only once in their last sixteen games of the season—the second leg of the Champions League semi-final against Chelsea at Stamford Bridge—and two goals on four occasions. In the rest of the eleven matches, they scored once or not at all.

This approach bore fruit as long as their defense was able to keep their opponents out, but when Real Madrid swarmed all over them, they actually ended up giving away their first Champions League title from a corner kick two minutes from time. When Sergio Ramos scored the equalizer in the Champions League final, Atlético didn't know what to do to score another goal and could only play for time in the hope of getting to penalties. Nothing in life is infallible, even that which seems perfect, and if you limit your resources, you'll give up the advantage.

But let us rewind a little. The 3-0 defeat against Osasuna in February with David Villa and Adrián in the starting lineup made Simeone see that after being given few opportunities, these two forwards now didn't respond when he needed them, because they weren't involved in the side's footballing dynamic.

Raúl García, in his season on loan, coincidentally at Osasuna, had changed from being a holding midfielder to an attacking midfielder and was very versatile and very consistent. Simeone had been using him like that and had dispensed with the services of Villa, Adrián, and "Cebolla" Rodríguez, three naturally attacking players.

After that defeat in Pamplona, Simeone gradually gave these three forwards more minutes, although it's also safe to assume that he felt he had to give the number of games Atlético played that season and the physical toll they took.

However, the job of replacing Diego Costa and Arda Turan in the Champions League final was too big for Villa and Adrián, as the rotation which had been forced on them over the season hadn't given them the experience of starting in a game of this magnitude. He had the raw material, but he hadn't been able to turn it into a product that was functional in all circumstances.

Simeone learned his lesson. After the "normal" 2014-2015 season, when they finished third in the league behind Barça and Real Madrid and were knocked out of the Champions League by their city rivals, in the 2015-2016 season Atlético were perhaps an even more effective version of themselves when Simeone showed that he'd identified the mistakes he had made two years before.

Now he used more nominal forwards; Griezmann and Torres learned to lead the line together as well as integrating perfectly into the side's defensive machinery. He didn't overload the midfield with Raúl García-type players, but instead used wingers like Yannick Ferreira Carrasco, and Saúl Ñíguez and Koke played behind the strikers. He also had the flexibility that Koke could either play higher up the pitch or in a double pivot with Gabi.

His players still didn't stop running and pressing. They all felt a part of the team's dynamic, and although there were some who were more regular starters than others, they all gave 100 percent when they came on. If all eleven had to defend, they did so, and they did it well. If they had to defend a one-goal lead, they all worked together, including the center forwards, without the more attack-minded players having to come off.

It wasn't an entirely defensive setup; Simeone knew that his formation and his players minimized the role luck plays in football, and he trusted in his own strengths. The defense conceded very few goals, and his forwards were capable of scoring goals from anywhere. It was a setup that rewarded sacrifice, and in the vast majority of matches it worked for him.

Simeone managed to get all his players to integrate in the squad and to make everyone feel important. Because it was such a demanding season, at the end of the day he was going to need them all. What could be better, then, than giving each player the right amount of responsibility so that each one understood his role and how to perform it?

Stefan Savić played for Diego Godín in the first leg of the Champions League semi-final against Bayern Munich and had an excellent game. Lucas Hernández played for José María Giménez against Barça in the previous round and played like a real veteran; Atlético didn't concede any goals and pushed the defending champions aside.

However, Simone still needs to evolve. He continues to fall victim to the dynamic that he drives himself and this consumes him. In the 2016 Champions League final against Real Madrid, he went for a more rigid and less mobile starting lineup, but a one-off game, especially a final, should not be prepared in the same way as a two-legged tie.

Simone stuck to the same formation that had worked against Barça and Bayern earlier in the competition, and it took him forty-five long minutes to change it. He put Augusto Fernández together with Gabi in defensive midfield and left the more attacking midfield areas for Koke and Saúl

Ñíguez, who do not have the pace to react quickly to Real Madrid's vertical and direct style.

In the run-in to the season, particularly in league games, Simeone was often forced to make the same change as he was at the break in that final because Atletico did not feel comfortable the way they were set up. He took off Augusto, pulled Koke back, and put Ferreira Carrasco on the wing to enhance their attacking options.

Real Madrid did not reach the end of that season with any kind of clear sense of identity or great self-confidence, and their patchy performance was evidence of this. This was the moment for Simeone to spring a surprise and release himself from the chains that had been holding him back, but he lacked the clarity to see how things might unfold and be able to take action before it was too late.

While Simeone should not be held 100 percent accountable because of the starting eleven he chose for the final, it is completely unforgivable that he did not exploit the emotional lift provided by the late equalizer to finish Real Madrid off in the last ten minutes. They were against the ropes, praying for the salvation of the full-time whistle, but he kept his substitutes on the bench. Why? It was as if he liked that masochistic game in which suffering and brutality emerged as the protagonists.

Real stayed alive because Atlético allowed them oxygen to breathe, and they ended up making off with the undécima because Simone was not able to release himself, to allow his metamorphosis, instead clinging to just one idea. To his idea.

He felt the setback deeply, and he realized that a large part of the responsibility for the defeat lay with him because immediately after the final he said he was considering whether to continue. It was a very bitter pill to swallow, and it was now so obvious though of course too late to try and change anything. Time will tell whether Simeone is able to escape from his self-imposed cell and find the balance on the other side of the barred windows.

What Mourinho and Simeone did brought them spectacular success and was more coherent, for example, than what Massimiliano Allegri tried to do with Juventus—the Italian champions and Champions League runners-up—in the Champions League 2015-2016 last sixteen return leg at Bayern Munich after a 2-2 draw in Turin.

Allegri played mainly with midfielders and defenders, with Álvaro Morata as a lone striker. They took an early 2-0 lead from two isolated attacks, but they never took a really active position; instead, they kept tight at the back and tried to play on the counter.

In the second half, Juventus made it easy for Bayern to lay siege to their goal because they posed no threat whatsoever in attack. As the saying goes, if at first you don't succeed, try, try again. That's what Bayern did, and they ended up winning the tie. Even if the result had been different, that's not a way worthy of a great team like Juventus to set up in a match against such a powerful opponent.

Allegri learned from his mistakes. The following season, he regularly started with Mario Mandžukić in a lineup that also included Paulo Dybala and Gonzalo Higuaín. Mandžukić was happy to play not as a center forward but farther back on the left, with more midfield responsibility and more involvement in defensive duties. His presence on the pitch allowed Juventus to defend with attackers and in turn to worry opposition defenses because of the number of forwards they needed to defend against. Allegri used these three players in both games against Barça and against Monaco in the Champions League, and they were easily the better team in both ties.

This isn't the only example of managers and teams who have failed in certain games and been defeated having set up the wrong way on the pitch; the list is very long. That's why Mourinho and Simeone clearly showed us that it's much better to defend with attackers than to attack with defenders.

Chapter 2

HOW TO EVOLVE WHILE STAYING TRUE TO YOURSELF

Around the middle of the last decade there seemed to be an increasing need among managers around Europe to play with a sole striker. To a large degree this epidemic was caused by the success achieved by Frank Rijkaard's Barcelona side, where Samuel Eto'o was the only out-and-out striker, although Ronaldinho and Ludovic Giuly first and Lionel Messi later also served as forwards.

More and more managers jumped on the bandwagon, only to find that its lack of original thought was to lead to failure. While at Barça there clearly wasn't just one forward, Didier Drogba was the only out-and-out striker in Mourinho's Chelsea. Joe Cole, a second striker, and Arjen Robben, a natural winger, were his partners in attack, and Mourinho built a team that was increasingly based on the strength of its midfield and on the finishing prowess of Drogba, although Frank Lampard's goal-scoring contribution was still invaluable.

Mourinho clung to that system and the team's impoverishment led to his being sacked, although Avram Grant managed to make a slightly better fist of it, righting the ship for the rest of the 2007-2008 season.

Scolari wanted to do the same thing, but his stubbornness and lack of flexibility soon meant he was shown the door at Stamford Bridge.

After his good 2007-2008 season with newly promoted Almería, and faced with the chaos Ronald Koeman had plunged Valencia into with his marginalization of Santiago Cañizares, David Albelda, and Miguel Ángel Angulo, the Valencia board decided to promote Unai Emery to its bench. It was a throw of the dice which in hindsight left Valencia in the same parlous footballing state it had been in the previous season.

Emery, just as Voro had done in the last games of the previous season after Koeman's sacking, put David Albelda back in midfield, but imposed a completely apathetic playing system.

Despite having Fernando Morientes in the squad, David Villa was the only first-choice forward. Joaquín played as a right winger, and the attack was completed by two men who played in the same position—David Silva and Juan Mata, who ended up getting in each other's way on the left-hand side. At times Silva was wrongly used in the middle since at that time he didn't have the skills he has now to play away from the wing. Because of this, Valencia finished outside the Champions League places that year.

Sir Alex Ferguson was one of those who, in response to continual European knockouts, started to change the way he approached difficult games, almost always when he was playing away from home. Faced with the increasing European trend of playing with just one up front, Ferguson realized that the antidote should be drawn from the poison itself.

So one of the last bastions of open, attacking football started not to be in certain games. If the opponent was playing with a 4–3–2–1 formation, or if it was a tough away game, Ferguson started to use the same system, and he got better results. So much so that after the 2003-2004 and 2004-2005 seasons, when Manchester United was knocked out of the Champions League at the last sixteen stage, and the 2005-2006 season when they finished bottom of a group containing Villarreal, Benfica, and Lille, in the next three seasons they reached two finals and were beaten in the semi-final by AC Milan in the other year.

At that time, teams used to approach games in the Premier League with the idea of going toe to toe with the opposition and trying to simply score more goals than them, with less caution and strategy. Obviously every game was worth the same as every other one; but in Europe, if your opponent sets up with a more cautious approach in a two-legged tie, it's going to be difficult to beat them unless you change your formation in some way, particularly if it's a strong team. However, there are exceptions; Mourinho's Inter won the Champions League in 2010, knocking out Chelsea and Barcelona on the way, with Sneijder and three forwards on the pitch, but this is very much the exception rather than the rule.

While Ferguson didn't make a habit of this practice, at times he did make a mistake deciding when to use it. In the run-in for the 2008-2009 season, after defeat by Liverpool at Old Trafford in the Premier League, the large lead United had enjoyed was whittled down to four potential points (they were one point ahead with a game in hand), and the hardest part of the season was coming up, with the final stretch of the Champions League, the FA Cup, and the league itself.

As well as the enormous quality of its players, one of the greatest strengths Manchester United had was the 4–4–2 Ferguson deployed in nine out of every ten matches. But that season, particularly in the second half of it, the presence of Dimitar Berbatov came to change his approach often, and that affected the Red Devils' style and power.

The Bulgarian usually started in the more important matches, but this wasn't proportionate with his displays, and certainly not with those of the man who was relegated to the bench, Carlos Tévez, a player who clicked perfectly with Wayne Rooney and Cristiano Ronaldo, the other two focal points of the United attack.

Tévez responded with fantastic goals on the rare chances he was given, but this wasn't enough for him to regain the key role he had played the season before.

On Sunday, May 10, he started the game and scored a great goal against Manchester City, but the following Wednesday he returned to the bench against Wigan, while Berbatov wandered around the pitch unnoticed. In the sixtieth minute, with United down 1-0, Tévez came on and within three minutes had scored the equalizer with a back heel out of nothing after a half chance for Carrick.

That was just one of several episodes where Manchester United took almost an hour to get into gear after an unproductive first half that had been dangerous in terms of their ambitions.

The first episode in this saga was the epic match against Aston Villa, where Ronaldo equalized in the eightieth minute and Federico Macheda scored the winner with a spectacular effort in added time, after allowing Martin O'Neill's team to seize the initiative and go up 2-1.

The second against Tottenham was no less momentous when they scored five goals in the second half having gone in at half-time down 2-0 at home, shaking themselves from a clearly torpid state.

The third was the game already mentioned against Wigan, a team who clearly came out to defend and who found themselves in front through a Hugo Rodallega goal following several slips by Nemanja Vidić. With Ronaldo quiet, Berbatov ineffective, and an excessive slowness in a midfield of Paul Scholes, Anderson, and Carrick, it had to be the latter with an incredible left-foot shot near the end after the Tevez equalizer to leave the league title within reach and finally lift the trophy the following Saturday against Arsenal at Old Trafford.

Perhaps if Ferguson had stuck to the natural 4–4–2 in the matches where he really needed to use it he would have kept the side's attacking threat and they wouldn't have had to work so hard against teams who didn't come close to matching the power of Manchester United.

The 3-0 victory against Chelsea with Fletcher as the only natural midfielder showed that tactical flexibility is the mother of success in football and is the best way to take all three points in an important game. However, you must have faith in the formation that brings you the best results, and in Manchester United's case, this was the one which had its attack as its first line of defense. Against the opposition of Aston Villa, Spurs, and Wigan, it made no sense to play with three holding midfielders.

Making the most of your greatest strength should always be your biggest priority, but many managers forget that to win games, while not conceding, you do have to score at least once.

In the summer of 2016, in his column in the *Telegraph*,[1] Carlo Ancelotti explained how France and Portugal should prepare for the European Championship final:

> *When a team reaches the final of one of the great summer tournaments – a World Cup, or a European Championship –*

> *the chances are that your players will be exhausted, their minds reeling at what can be accomplished, and as a manager you can only try to keep it simple.*

And he added:

> *The important thing is to focus on the strengths that you have in your own team. Remind the players of the strategy that has seen them through the tournament so well up until that point. Talk about their own qualities and how they can win. You need to give your players confidence and try to make sure they can do all the good things that got them into this position in the first place.*

Although the Champions League final is a little different to the tournaments Ancelotti was referring to, there are also certain similarities. They are played at the end of the season, when fatigue weighs heavier than ever and the team has acquired a real winning mentality that has allowed them to qualify for such an exclusive match. It's rare that an unstable team with issues of identity has made it through. Perhaps Chelsea in 2012 and Real Madrid in 2016 are the most recent examples.

It is, therefore, a question of allowing the dynamic achieved over the course of nearly nine months of work to take hold of the team—without abandoning the need to cancel out your opponent's strengths and enhance your own—when the time comes to define everything you have worked so hard for.

In the 2009 Champions League final, Ferguson was more worried about stopping Barça from playing their natural game than getting his own team to play theirs, and he paid for it with defeat. It was obviously going to be very difficult to stop Barcelona from bringing the ball out and attacking as they always did. But to sit back and play long balls out wasn't really a logical solution because it gave no guarantee of scoring a goal or two. With the number of goals the Catalans scored that season, it was going to be almost impossible to hope for a positive outcome based on keeping a clean sheet.

Putting pressure on the ball high up with aggressive marking might have paid dividends, but for the whole match Ferguson was unable to come up with an approach that found weaknesses in the formidable Barcelona tactical formation.

Carrick and Anderson started as holding midfielders, but the latter hadn't been involved in the most important matches of the season. You can rotate players in all competitions and matches, but your starting lineup must be carefully chosen in the difficult games. Scholes, because of his experience, years of service, and footballing prowess was more suited to a Champions League final.

Giggs had been played in the double pivot several times—for example in the 3-0 win against Chelsea—and now he decided to put him into that area to help bring the ball forward a bit better, particularly with long balls, but his duties were basically more defensive. Park Ji-sung performed a similar job, while Rooney and Ronaldo tried to create what they could when they got the ball, but they were never able to attack in an organized manner and in numbers, which was always one of Manchester United's best weapons. It was impossible to even think of achieving any kind of coherence like that against the Barça steamroller.

In the second half and more because of the disastrous play by his team than the narrow score line against them, Sir Alex Ferguson decided to take Anderson off and put Tévez on. This turned out to be too abrupt a change because he needed to keep the defensive midfield solidity, and the Brazilian was providing that more than Ryan Giggs. If Park had been the player taken off, the team left on the pitch would have had Carrick and Anderson in midfield and Giggs, Ronaldo, Rooney, and Tévez up front, which would have been very similar to how United had played on countless occasions that season.

With a little tactical organization, certain precautions to prevent being left exposed at the back and to form a resolute attacking mentality, destiny may have been changed. But the desperate changes Ferguson made weren't the intelligent ones that the situation required.

Ronaldo and Tévez blamed Sir Alex Ferguson for not being so attack-minded from the start: "We didn't do well. The tactics were not good and everything went wrong for us. We were only in it for 10 minutes, and we never found ourselves again."[2] The Argentine admitted that he should have had more time on the pitch, but at the end of the day it wasn't up to him. As could be seen, even the players themselves didn't feel comfortable with the way Ferguson set the team up in Rome on May 27.

César Luis Menotti, Argentina's world champion manager in 1978, described Ferguson's attitude delightfully while at the same time highlighting the sensational football played by the team he once managed: "*Barça's play was so honest and brilliant that always annihilated any attempt at not playing,*"[3] and this was due in no small part to the fact that Guardiola remained faithful to his style. The more difficult the opponent is, the more you have to stick to what has brought you such success. In a final, you can't disguise yourself so much because you'll end up confusing yourself.

The following year, in 2010, Manchester United had just a week and three games at the end of March and the beginning of April to save their whole season. The two Champions League quarter-final games against Bayern Munich sandwiched the small matter of the "league final" against Chelsea at Old Trafford.

In the first leg, Bayern was powerless to penetrate the United defense. However, they somehow managed, half by luck and half by perseverance, to score two goals near the end, win the match 2-1, and force the Red Devils to work a bit harder in the return leg, for which Rooney was a major doubt after injuring his ankle right at the end of the match.

The match against Chelsea the following weekend showed the severe dependence on Rooney of a team that was lost in attack and a Dimitar Berbatov who was even more lost, having been preferred by Ferguson to Carlos Tévez, who had left the summer before.

Manchester United hadn't shown such a lack of football for a long time; they'd been weakened by Ferguson's belief that he could go through the whole season with just a few forwards in Rooney, Berbatov, Michael Owen, and occasional cameos from Federico Macheda and Danny Welbeck, who had gone to Preston on loan in January.

Chelsea stayed calm, trusted in the power of their players, and was helped by the obvious ineffectiveness of Manchester United; Joe Cole's back-heel put them on easy street very early on.

It wasn't just the tactics offered by Ferguson that were wrong, but also the attitude of the team in the first half, when they were completely caught up in a bland, vague style of play with their players wandering aimlessly around the pitch.

That day, Ferguson rested players for the Champions League return leg against Bayern. He left Nani and Carrick on the bench and delegated defensive midfield responsibilities to Paul Scholes, Darren Fletcher, and Ryan Giggs. Fletcher was his great man in the middle of the pitch, with a remarkable freedom and performance. He defended, but he also joined the attack and put precise crosses in.

But in this game Fletcher was too committed to defense and rarely got forward, while Giggs created nothing in the final third and was far from being a defensive wall. In the second half, the side's attitude improved considerably, and they really went for the win, but it wasn't enough. Chelsea had too much testosterone and their football was too good to allow it. Berbatov wouldn't have scored that day even if he had been playing against Scunthorpe reserves. They ended up losing 2-1 and were overtaken at the top of the league. They were never to regain the lead.

Nobody knows how, but after the medical team announced that Rooney's injury would keep him out for a month, he miraculously started the return leg against Bayern just four days after he limped off against Chelsea. In his book *Leading*, which was published years later, Sir Alex Ferguson revealed that he asked Rooney to continue to wear the protective boot to pretend that he was really injured and to confuse Bayern.

The match started perfectly; they scored twice in the first ten minutes, and Bayern was rattled. Then the third goal went in, and, although they weren't overconfident, everything seemed to be settled until Ivica Olić's goal at the end of the first half struck fear into their bones.

Rafael's foolish red card left them exposed, and Manchester United was cornered, dominated, and defenseless.

But again, Bayern's perseverance, Robben's individual brilliance, and the left-foot shot he fired past Edwin van der Sar forced Ferguson to accept responsibility for the situation. Before that goal, when Bayern was camped around the Manchester United area, Ferguson made a serious mistake.

Often when the opposition was pressing, this brilliant Scottish manager used to make attacking changes that would punish them and release any pressure United was under. That was one of his great qualities, showing that to protect a lead you didn't need to replace forwards with defenders, but could do quite the opposite.

Manchester United was winning 3-1 and was still ahead in the tie, but when Bayern threw itself desperately forward to get the second goal, the best thing Ferguson could have done was to attack them relentlessly, so that the German side felt uncomfortable both tactically and mentally.

Rooney's ankle couldn't be relied on to charge forward against Bayern, and he couldn't be pushed too much. So the most obvious thing was to substitute him for another attacker. The presence of a more in-form forward and perhaps an additional attacking substitution might have brought the goal they needed to breathe more easily, or he might also have gone for more and better possession of the ball.

But he didn't. Ten minutes into the second half, he took Rooney off and brought on John O'Shea—a defender! This smoothed the way for Bayern to achieve some coherence when they were allowed to, but who were certainly not the paradigm of a solid team.

Robben scored the goal that turned the tie on its head, and with ten minutes to go—just ten—Ferguson remembered about Berbatov. However, it would have been an ironic twist of fate indeed if the Bulgarian had needed so little time to do what he hadn't managed to do all season.

It's like if you behave in a particular way your whole life because you're sure that's the right way to do it, but then one fine day, for no apparent reason, you decide to behave entirely differently. Obviously, you can't. It can all be traced back to Tévez's departure and the perhaps inevitable exit of Cristiano Ronaldo, and up to an exclusive dependence on Rooney to suffocate opposition defenses and, to a large extent, to score goals.

He thought that without Ronaldo and Tévez he would be able to make a team just as strong. Well, without Ronaldo, because he had barely used Tévez the season before, the team had become a group of players of more or less the same level without any fixed starters. Just as the departure of Ferguson in 2013 destabilized the team, after Ronaldo left for Real Madrid in 2009, United had a flat season.

On the other hand, when Carlo Ancelotti arrived at Chelsea, he radically changed his ideas from his last period at AC Milan and turned them into a serious and, above all, attacking side. In order to understand why he abandoned his old ideas, let's make use an analogy of everyday life.

When two people meet, at first they behave formally toward each other, keeping up as austere a front as possible. As they begin to feel more comfortable with each other, whether it's a work relationship or they're friends or partners, they each start to discover who the other person really is.

Ancelotti was somebody who had AC Milan in his veins, and he was given a certain leeway, if we can put it like that, to impose his own ideas, even though not all were to the liking of Silvio Berlusconi and Adriano Galliani.

At Chelsea, he had to do things as tastefully as possible, at least at the start, which is why he adopted a very attacking style for almost his first whole season. As might be expected, his results were excellent, and he won the Premier League and the FA Cup. It was an evolution that was similar to Mourinho when he arrived at Inter: Both were very different from their pasts.

Indeed, in an interview published by the newspaper *La Repubblica*[4] in 2009, Ancelotti admitted that he'd abandoned the tactical inflexibility from his first steps in management and had become a flexible manager.

The influence of Arrigo Sacchi when he was starting out had made him adopt a very closed approach, but he didn't mind publicly showing his evolution:

> *When I started I was too "Sacchi-like," and I only used a 4–4–2. With Sacchi it had been very successful, and I was afraid of change. I never signed Roberto Baggio because a number 10 did not fit with my formation. I let Gianfranco Zola go when he was competing with Hernán Crespo and Enrico Chiesa for a place in the Parma side. Today I would keep Zola and I would tell Baggio: "I'm waiting for you." At Juventus I had Zidane, and I did not make the same mistakes as I did at Parma. At AC Milan I had to work out how Pirlo, Seedorf, Rui Costa, and Rivaldo could play together. Football today has two things which you can't do without: a striker who scores goals and the return of a "trequartista" who can play between the lines. Now I only stick to the back four. From the midfield forwards you can do anything.*

Seven years later, in exclusive comments on the website *Goal,*[5] Ancelotti confirmed this:

> *The first time that I met Zinedine Zidane was in my first year in Juventus, and I found a fantastic player. Zidane was the key for me to change my idea of football because I was always used to playing 4–4–2.*
>
> *At Juventus I changed my system, to play a player like him behind two strikers because I didn't want to change his position. He was really fantastic.*

Changing tactics from one season to the next is necessary not just to avoid being too predictable for your opponents, but also to keep the players on their toes in terms of their levels of performance.

That's what Mourinho did at Porto in 2003 after winning the league, Cup, and UEFA Cup treble to stop his players becoming complacent—so they didn't start thinking they were unbeatable—and the following year he achieved even better results, winning the league and the Champions League.

Sir Alex Ferguson elaborated on this in the 2015-2016 Champions League technical report. Talking about Barça and the need to continue to evolve in order to maintain domestic and European dominance, Ferguson said that "*where they had had a carousel of possession with no central striker they now have three excellent front strikers* [Messi, Suárez, and Neymar] *and play far more positively in terms of penetration. They're still looking for a different way of playing*."[6]

Antonio Conte will need to carry out some kind of tactical change in the 3–4–3 approach that made Chelsea more stable and led to their winning the Premier League in the 2016-2017 season. He doesn't necessarily have to abandon the idea of playing with three center backs, as he's shown that he's very skillful when it comes to building a solid defense with that formation—but not so much with a back four—but sooner or later opponents will find a way of making them less impenetrable. The change might take place in midfield, or on the flanks, a new strategy which might motivate his players and provide them with a different plan to continue to be as successful as they were in Conte's first season at Chelsea.

At Barça, something similar happened. In Luis Enrique's final season there was a significant tactical deterioration in the team and a lack of motivation in the manager and in his players to maintain the same level as in the previous two seasons. The footballing dip—a completely normal occurrence—created a psychological dip, and that psychological dip grew to the point where it closed the circle and became responsible for the footballing dip. That's what Luis Enrique shouldn't have allowed.

With Guardiola in his first season at Manchester City, the first of these things happened but not completely the second.

Messi, as the team's axis, may be the key to the tactical changes Ernesto Valverde should introduce and might cause the performance levels of all those top players to take off again so that their sum is even greater than their parts.

Messi worked fantastically well when he played as a false 9 with Guardiola, and playing him there again might stimulate him tactically as well as creating a new dynamic in the team's midfield, something Barça is crying out for. This would also cause more uncertainty in their opponents, because if the replacements for Messi, Neymar, and Luis Suárez are quite different from one another when the attacking moves start, it will be more chaotic for defenses trying to control them all. If they get together to finish the attack and Messi appears in the area to apply the finishing touches with short and impulsive runs, very few teams will be able to deal successfully with his finishing ability. The solution is not to put any player at the service of Messi, but to put everyone at the service of the most important thing, the team, with an already tried and tested tactical variation.

HOW FERGUSON WENT BACK TO HIS ROOTS AND BETRAYED THEM AGAIN

In the 2010-2011 season, Manchester United benefited from Chelsea's unexpected slump in form between November and December, but they weren't a completely solid team. They drew a lot of games—particularly away from home—and Rooney didn't score many goals, although his form gradually improved, and by the end of the season he was the same fantastic player as always. However, he contributed more to the build-up play, to working hard, and to a new role of box-to-box midfielder, but not as much to scoring goals.

Nevertheless, the battle against Ancelotti's Chelsea went beyond the Premier League and was also decisive in the Champions League. At that time, they were the only two teams capable of fighting for the Premier League title and the only serious English contenders in Europe.

Manchester United had already beaten Chelsea in the Community Shield, but in their first Premier League meeting of the season, played on March 1, Chelsea gained revenge with a 2-1 victory at Stamford Bridge.

One month later came that frenetic meeting in the Champions League quarter-final, and Ferguson needed to plan a surprise to come up with something to thwart the cunning plans Ancelotti would design for the tie.

Manchester United won both games, like that 3-0 in January 2009, by playing with one holding midfielder, Carrick, and five attackers. Of course, when Chelsea got the ball back, Carrick wasn't left on his own in the middle of the pitch; he had help mainly from Giggs and Park, but it remained a clearly offensive formation. This was another example of the benefits of defending with attackers.

In their second and decisive Premier League meeting, Sir Alex Ferguson repeated the formation and, with the help of two serious mistakes by Chelsea, made sure the league title would go back to Old Trafford. So, why did he use this system and why did it work so well for him?

In that Premier League defeat in March, Ferguson used Carrick, Scholes, and Fletcher in midfield, while the attack was made up of Nani, Rooney, and Javier Hernández. Chelsea was more comfortable on the pitch, while Manchester United found it hard to play coherent attacking football.

But now Ferguson decided to gamble on mobile players in midfield who were not so defensive—except Carrick—but who were quicker when it came to the transition to attack. How did he offset this? By making them drop back when the team lost the ball. Chicharito was the only one who stayed up all the time.

The key for this plan was the lightning speed with which the ball was brought forward once it had been won. Chelsea didn't have time to reorganize at the back and was completely scattered when they ran back. Breakdown of the risks and benefits: fewer specialists in recovering the ball, but more mobility and effectiveness in moving it and building play.

What did he come up with to contain the Chelsea attack? He took advantage of the speed of his attacking players to close down a team that played quick, one-touch football, looking for gaps and little balls through.

A solid back line was led by Nemanja Vidić and Rio Ferdinand, and there was a second line of five or six who organized quickly and blocked off the possible passes to the point that when the Chelsea players got the ball they were so tightly marked they barely had time to turn toward goal or to make two or three passes safely in the final third. They were allowed to come forward so far, but not to get past.

In the second Premier League game in May, he kept the five attackers on at all times and won the match 2-1. Revenge is a dish best served cold. Here, it was the dish of champions.

However, this wasn't the Manchester United who had won three league titles in a row with Ronaldo and who had been proclaimed European champions. If Chelsea hadn't had that dip at the end of the year perhaps it would have been a different story. They weren't a high definition team, but they were the best standard definition team. Being the least bad is another way of being the best. Sir Alex Ferguson found an effective way of counteracting their opponent's strengths and of enhancing those of his team, and he did it brilliantly.

But while this formation worked against Chelsea, it needed to be applied selectively, not blindly. The opponent you're facing will make you change your ideas and will force you to find a way which is similar, but not the same, to achieve victory.

Ferguson needed to bring something unexpected to the table to beat Barça in the Champions League final, the second between these two teams in just three years. He needed three aces up his sleeve and another two up his trouser leg. The old formula of putting men behind the ball was the most effective against the Catalan team, but that wasn't his style. The pressure more than warranted it, and there would have been no shame in doing this with all his players, but the key lay in deciding which men to use and how to play with them. The lineup which worked so well against Chelsea would be swept aside like a Sunday league side by Guardiola's team. He couldn't risk playing it.

But that's what he did, and they were only able to give as good as they got for the first fifteen minutes. His lineup didn't have the motivation or the skill to keep up the pressure and keep pain at bay. Neither Ferguson nor his players knew what to do once Barça had settled into the game and started to impose their style of play. It's like chess: You have to play keeping in mind the possible moves your opponent might make and the moves you'll make next in reaction to what your opponent has done.

It's not like American football, where you defend with a different team from the one you attack with. Instead, it's more like other sports, where you must design a double strategy for the same players.

As this lineup wasn't equipped to deal with the opposition dominating possession to such an extent, they ended up defending deep in order not to be exposed, and even then they were left looking naked for the first two Barcelona goals.

Ferguson must have felt sure that the Manchester United team didn't have many weapons with which to defeat a team as solid as Barça. If he knew his team and its weak points, and he also knew the opposition well, he should have known that United would be defending more than they would be attacking, so his lineup, without losing much of its attacking threat, should have been set up to contain the storm that was going to break around it.

Against Chelsea the lineup with five attacking players worked because Ancelotti's side didn't have the same quality when in possession and weren't tactically as well prepared as Barça. The defense in those two games was much more disciplined, and the spaces between the lines were minimal. Unthinkably, the back line of the midfield against Barça, which wasn't even straight, left an enormous space behind it through which Xavi was able to run into whenever he wished and which meant that Messi was able to shoot from the edge of the area for the second goal without being closed down.

It was fine for the Chelsea game, but this approach should have been customized. It was easy to see that it wasn't going to work against Barça.

Ferguson opted for a mediocre Javier Hernández in that season's run-in, but he didn't score many goals, was always getting caught offside, and didn't contribute to the team's play. The Champions League final was the ideal match for him not to play, particularly given the nature of the opposition, as it was clear that he brought absolutely nothing; this was a match where Ferguson needed to be given the very best by all his players.

Interestingly, in this final, maybe it was the right thing to start with Anderson in place of Darren Fletcher, who, before his stomach problems had taken him out of the team for two months, had provided that essential balance between defensive duties and those of organizing attacks, and he had been one of the players who made the difference for Manchester United in the difficult games.

Perhaps the ideal starting lineup would have been with Carrick and Anderson in midfield, Park, Giggs, and Nani—not Valencia—a little higher up, and Rooney as striker. This was perhaps a better way to hold on with a bit more presence in the midfield but still have the weapons necessary to hurt Barcelona when they got the ball. If you make your players play defensively and they don't have, for example, the mentality of Simeone's Atlético team, they're not going to know what to do with the ball when they get it.

Ferguson opted for Luis Antonio Valencia because he defends better than Nani, but if he'd reinforced his defensive midfield with Anderson, then he would have been able to give a little more freedom to his more attacking players. Playing with just one holding midfielder against a team that dominates possession as much as Barça is clearly suicide, and the absence of Fletcher was a major disaster.

Nani could have been more effective as a winger because of his speed, his touch, his dribbling, and especially his long-range shooting—a weapon Manchester United was going to need to use a lot.

Chapter 3

CONCERNING E(IN)VOLUTION

Talking about Arsène Wenger and Arsenal can be as tedious as the club's present situation. It's a situation that stretches back over several years since the new stadium's debt was paid off; the guidance of the club's longstanding manager has robbed it of its capacity to stir feelings of ecstasy again in fans who have now lost faith. Part of the legacy of Arsène Wenger lies in the sporting and commercial success which allowed Arsenal to move to its new, modern Emirates Stadium. Cheap signings, players sold for a lot of money, and the trophies in the early years meant Highbury was too small a home, and the years of financial and therefore footballing limitations were inevitable. In post-modern football, except in very exceptional and rare cases, success comes hand in hand with money. Leicester City is the exception to this rule.

But once that necessary period of paying off the stadium had ended, despite many of his decisions in those gray years, and although his time at Arsenal is not yet over, it is difficult to assess the net effect of his tenure, qualitatively speaking.

Moving to the Emirates Stadium was, without doubt, an important step that other big clubs such as Chelsea, Liverpool, and Tottenham Hotspur took later or are yet to take and was made possible by Wenger's fabulous management in his first years at the club. But the rest matters.

Probably no other club and no other manager would have been able to keep a team permanently among the top four in England with a salary cap of just five figures per week in the years following a ground change. The question is, what was the price, globally, that the club paid for the Emirates Stadium?

Many things people blame Wenger for today weren't the fruit of the financial pressures resulting from the debt repayment, but were born of his inability to get the best out of the squads he's managed. If Wenger had done many things differently, even if Arsenal had gone through the same period without winning important trophies, there wouldn't be the same number of voices complaining about his stubbornness and demanding he leave.

Wenger constantly changes lineups and formations, both within the same season and from season to season. Sometimes he takes a liking to a particular established player, and he never takes him off; at other times he does the same thing with a young player fresh out of the youth academy, even when the player's form is not the most consistent. Arsenal is always a team permanently under construction, and he continues to repeat the same mantra: "We have shown in the last weeks that we can do great things, and we have to try to keep this run going." But he doesn't see that those spells are just that—runs—and Arsenal is still caught in the same vicious circle that ends in mediocrity, season after season, even though there are moments like the end of the 2016-2017 season that provide a certain amount of hope.

Wenger seems engrossed in that permanent endeavor of finding the formation and the players that work best for him. He can never stick with a stable approach because the dressing room changes so much; his top players always end up leaving, and the injuries keep coming thick and fast. He goes from day to day trying things out to see what works best.

In the 2010-2011 Champions League tie against Barça, after winning the first leg 2-1, Arsène Wenger used five central midfielders in the return leg and left Robin van Persie on his own up front. Against Barça you're not going to have many chances, and you need to take advantage of the ones you get. With that lineup, it was impossible to get anything out of the game at the Camp Nou.

Arsenal "scored" a Sergio Busquets own goal and didn't have a shot on goal all night. Of course, they had Van Persie very unfairly sent off, but even when they were playing with eleven men they did nothing. Wenger should have assumed that Barcelona would score, and he needed to be prepared for the worst. To get through, they couldn't play for a goalless draw, as it was very unlikely they would get one.

Quite apart from the difference in squads, that game showed Arsène Wenger's fear and the lack of nous he has when facing an important tie against a difficult opponent.

Despite having to defend with all his men and the fact that throwing men behind the ball might have been part of the solution—a large part—he needed to attack, and he had to do it with forwards, not midfielders. No two games are ever the same, and even if you hang from the crossbar, you might end up conceding fifteen goals.

Whereas other clubs have too little patience with some players, Wenger is the exact opposite. It's not that Olivier Giroud is a bad player; it's just that he's made it clear that no team will win a competitive league like the Premier League with him as their center forward. To make matters worse, Danny Welbeck (in 2014) and Alexandre Lacazette (in 2017) were the only center forwards signed by Wenger, but Welbeck doesn't have the influence to achieve what the team needs, and Lacazette's performances remain to be seen. Walcott is a useful player to have, but he's not going to score twenty-five goals a season. Then in the 2016-2017 season Wenger decided to redesign his attack without a clear number 9, and although Alexis Sánchez scored twenty-four goals in the Premier League, that wasn't enough to even remain in the top four.

Perhaps Arsenal wouldn't need to work so hard at building such an elaborate and elegant style of play in midfield with subtle playmakers like Santi Cazorla and Mesut Özil, if up front he had a Van Nistelrooy, a Tévez, or a Zlatan. But they still don't have a proper goal poacher, and Wenger doesn't seem too interested in finding one.

The same thing has happened in midfield. Alexandre Song left in 2012 on the last day of the transfer window, and there was no time to find a replacement. This was one of the worst transfers in Arsenal's recent history, not just because of the quality of the player they lost, but because of the timing of his being allowed to leave the club.

Wenger had to move Mikel Arteta back to the base of the midfield for the rest of the season, and the following summer he still didn't bring in a specialist in that position. It wasn't until the emergence of Francis Coquelin in the 2014-2015 season that he could play somebody whose natural position was just in front of the back line. Even then, in the 2015-2016 season, when Coquelin was injured, he found it very hard to put his faith in Mathieu Flamini.

The example of the Barça game is not the only one where Arsène Wenger didn't choose the best lineup for a particular game. Sometimes his whims lead to him sticking with a good player who wasn't in good form—as he had for certain periods of time with Mesut Özil—or marginalizing another player who was crying out for an opportunity to show his worth, as he did with Joel Campbell.

In the 2013-2014 season Arsenal faced Bayern Munich in the last sixteen of the Champions League. Around then the story emerged of the woman Olivier Giroud took into the hotel where the team was staying. Wenger wanted to make an example of Giroud by leaving him on the bench against Bayern, but who would replace him? Yaya Sanogo!

Whatever Olivier Giroud may do or not do in his private life, even if it was during the team's prematch build-up, the answer wasn't to leave him on the bench in a key game because then it's the team that is affected. The attacking options, because of Arsenal's inability to sign another competent center forward, were far from extensive enough to do away with the services of his only natural number 9.

The club's pride should come before all else, and anything which goes against it is unacceptable. Wenger ended up harming the club by wanting to make an example of a player.

In that same game, and not because he missed a penalty but because of his characteristics and his recent performances, Mesut Özil shouldn't have started. Perhaps he was very tired after being an ever-present that season, or maybe he was going through a mini-crisis, which is quite normal, it happens to almost every player. In his place, Tomáš Rosický or Lukas Podolski would have been a better option because of their greater contribution to both defense and attack in a game where Arsenal would need to strengthen with players who could perform both functions.

Another player who shouldn't have started was Jack Wilshere, but he did so along with Özil, and Wenger condemned his team from the moment he decided on his starting eleven. They lost 0-2 at home, and in the return leg, although Giroud did start, there was no coming back.

Arsène Wenger's fear of managing a lead with a balanced lineup is another of his most visible flaws. In the 2015-2016 season—when he had a golden opportunity to win the Premier League because of Chelsea's terrible start and Manchester United's and Manchester City's lack of stability—his deepest-held fears came to the surface.

On December 21, Arsenal played Manchester City in one of the potential championship deciders. At that point, nobody believed Leicester would keep going until May.

Alexis Sánchez, Danny Welbeck, Santi Cazorla, and Francis Coquelin were all injured. Wenger played with Mathieu Flamini and Aaron Ramsey in midfield, and Mesut Özil, Joel Campbell, and Theo Walcott behind Olivier Giroud. A very coherent, balanced, and attacking lineup.

Walcott and Giroud scored in the first half, and Arsenal was about to spring a surprise. Until that moment.

In the second half Manchester City threw everything at the Arsenal goal, and Wenger's knees began to tremble. In the seventieth minute, he took Campbell off and put on Kieran Gibbs, a full back. Fifteen minutes later he made an even more defensive change, putting on Calum Chambers for Theo Walcott. Manchester City had already scored once and were laying siege to Petr Cech's goal.

By pure luck, they didn't score a second, but that didn't hide the fact that Wenger wasn't used to managing a lead without retreating to his burrow. When the opponent presses, he gives them the ball and plays a real nineteenth-century style of football, like the one Mourinho criticized

Sam Allardyce for once. Wenger calls that "*knowing how to deal with the pressure,*" as he put it after the game.[7]

Some days before, he had explained why Olivier Giroud had been temporarily left out of the team. "*Forwards suffer a lot of wear and tear. They need a rest, to come in and out of the team. I think I will do it* [leave him out of some games] *again during the season,*" he said.[8]

So does this mark a shift in his views on this subject?

Thierry Henry, his first-choice center forward for the eight seasons he played for the Gunners, played over thirty games in the Premier League alone in each of those seasons except in the last one when injuries didn't allow it. Robin van Persie didn't play more when Henry left only because he was beset by injuries, but even then, in his last season (2011-2012) he played all thirty-eight Premier League games and did so again in his first season at Manchester United. Sir Alex Ferguson never talked about it and never complained about wear and tear. So how come Wenger now needed to ration the time Giroud played in in the key matches of the season? He was his only available center forward!

But that example against Manchester City wasn't an isolated incident. It's very common to see Wenger make defensive changes toward the end of a game if he has a lead of one or two goals.

In the 2010-2011 season at Everton, Arsenal were up 2-0 after forty-eight minutes. He'd started with Andrei Arshavin and Marouane Chamakh up front but ended up substituting them for Tomáš Rosický and Emmanuel Eboué. Tim Cahill scored for Everton near the end, and Arsenal ended the game praying for the final whistle with their goal under siege and very close to surrendering their lead. Any team that claims to be great can't project an image like that.

On the other hand, when Arsenal goes behind, which happens quite regularly, then just the opposite happens. He takes his deeper-lying players off the pitch and floods it with forwards.

Curiously, in the second game against Everton that season, we saw the other side of the coin. He started with Alexandre Song, Tomáš Rosický, Francesc Fàbregas, and Jack Wilshere in midfield—four players with similar central midfield characteristics—but because Everton went ahead in the first half, after the break Arsène Wenger completely changed tack.

He had started with Theo Walcott and Robin van Persie up front, but he now gave them the support of Arshavin and Nicklas Bendtner. Of the four central midfield players who started, only Fàbregas ended the game. That afternoon had a happy ending because Arsenal ended up winning 2-1 with a goal by Arshavin and another from Laurent Koscielny from a corner.

But why does Arsène Wenger change his mind so quickly and so radically? Wasn't that the ideal starting eleven to get a victory with? So why did he change it like that? Too many questions requiring, but not finding, a logical answer.

Arsenal's image on the continent has been completely eroded. Lionel Messi, after Barcelona's win at the Emirates Stadium in the Champions League last sixteen meeting in 2016, said this: "*We knew that Arsenal would not be able to last the whole game*."[9]

That's how Barça prepared for the game, like a beast waiting for the right moment to finish its prey off, in no hurry because it knows that sooner or later it will fall into the trap of its own accord.

How can Arsène Wenger motivate his players now? What arguments can he use to get more from every one of his players and take them beyond their basic performance level? The continual repetition of bitter seasons of frustration has pierced the dressing room morale deeply, and they can't reach the level of mental strength needed to build a solid footballing machine. If you are mentally strong, you can be physically and tactically strong, but without that mental strength, it's unlikely.

In the 2016-2017 season, on February 11 against Hull City, Mesut Özil missed a clear chance and immediately kicked the air in a clear act of frustration. That act showed how Wenger is unable to give the right emotional guidance to his players. You can make a mistake—even Messi and Ronaldo do—but you have to keep your head up when it happens in order to keep playing your best.

The peak of Arsène Wenger's lack of understanding came in the 2015-2016 season, when he complained about the poor support from the fans after being eliminated from the Champions League by Barcelona and the FA Cup by Watford. "*What hurts me is that at the important moment of the season we played in a skeptical environment.* [Criticism] *from the media, OK. From our fans? It is a bit more difficult to take*," he said.[10]

Wenger still doesn't realize that the club's supporters, the real supporters, are fed up with so much mediocrity and so much anxiety. The new stadium was paid for several years ago, and Arsenal has spent 40 million on Mesut Özil and Alexis Sánchez and now offer competitive salaries, but they've had to settle for just three FA Cups.

The final twist of the story came in the same season when he said that Arsenal had let the Premier League title escape at home against weaker opposition because of the lack of support from the fans. No, Arsène, the lack of support isn't toward the team, the club, or the players, it's toward you and the club's weak board.

Three weeks after that game against Hull City, on March 4, in an exclusive interview with *BT Sport* aired the day Arsenal lost at Anfield while Alexis Sánchez was left on the bench and with the fans' dissatisfaction reaching uncharted levels, Wenger said that he'd been a manager since he was thirty-three and that in all that time nobody had questioned his authority, but now, at the age of sixty-seven, people were wondering whether he was up to the job.[11]

He also said that he felt able to lead the club to a higher level, but that the reason he hadn't succeeded in doing it that season was that people hadn't stopped criticizing him. At the end of the season he repeated that Arsenal had played a lot of home games in a very hostile atmosphere.

In summer 2013 the Arsenal Supporters' Trust (AST) issued a statement, declaring that, in a survey, 80 percent of fans who voted said they were in favor of Wenger continuing, but thought that the manager had too much control over transfer fees.

They also recommended that the board shouldn't rush to renew Wenger's contract and should first consider that season's results. In the end, Arsenal ended their nine-year drought by lifting the FA Cup, and Wenger's contract was renewed for three more seasons.

The AST also nearly unanimously requested junior members should join the club's board of directors and even supported Wenger forming part of it. They declared:

> *The Arsenal Board needs some dynamic younger members and greater diversity so that it represents the club's playing personnel and supporters.*[12]

They also asked for Stan Kroenke, the majority shareholder, to explain his vision for the club. They were starting to question the owner's commitment. Weeks later, despite the club spending 42.5 million pounds (approximately 55 million dollars) to sign Mesut Özil, they were worried about so few of the reserves of money in the club being used to improve the squad.

The statement read:

> *Arsenal supporters are dismayed by this continued lack of ambition, most notably illustrated when the manager describes fourth place as like a trophy. We do not advocate reckless spending for the sake of it; we advocate proper use of all of the available resources for the benefit of the team.*[13]

In the summer of 2015, after Arsène Wenger had only signed Petr Cech and no outfield players, the AST used a stronger tone to go on the charge again. In a meeting with AST and Arsenal's chief executive, Ivan Gazidis, they demanded that the club directors review Wenger's transfer policy:

> *This isn't an issue that affects just one transfer window and seems to indicate a wider structural issue. In recent years Arsenal have overhauled both their Academy and their medical set-up. We urge the board to now open a full review into its arrangements for scouting and purchasing players. A review of this type can only help Arsenal to become a stronger club.*[14]

Two weeks later, the publication of the club's balance sheet showed that they had nearly 200 million pounds (approximately 260 million dollars) available, something which infuriated the supporters still more. Around that time, Arsenal had been defeated by Dynamo Zagreb in the first match in the group stage of the Champions League.

In February 2016, the highly respected blog *The Swiss Ramble* —written by the Gunners fan Kieron O'Connor—mentioned again the vast financial resources available to Arsenal (159 million pounds) after they had only bought the Egyptian midfielder Mohamed Elneny in the January transfer window.

Apart from the familiar undemanding nature of the club's directors, why have Arsenal's consistent failures not resulted in Wenger's departure?

Until now, despite supporters' dissatisfaction reaching its peak in 2017, Arsenal has alternated "successes" with "failures" cyclically.

For example, in the 2009-2010 season, Manchester United and Chelsea were the only Premier League title contenders; Arsenal finished third, but never mounted a challenge to the leaders **(BAD)**. The following season they reached the League Cup final **(GOOD)**, but lost against Birmingham City with a defensive horror show in the final **(BAD)**. In the last games in the Premier League, Manchester City snatched third place from them and forced Arsenal to play in the qualification stage of the Champions League **(BAD)**. There, they faced a very strong team in Udinese, but they won both legs **(GOOD)**.

In the 2011-2012 season, they started poorly in the league **(BAD)**, but they won their Champions League group **(GOOD)**. AC Milan thrashed them 4-0 in the first leg of their last sixteen tie **(BAD)**, but two weeks later they won at Anfield **(GOOD)**.

In the return leg against AC Milan they scored three goals in the first half, and the comeback seemed within reach **(GOOD)**, but they didn't score again and were knocked out **(BAD)**.

They were no longer in contention for the league, the Champions League, or either domestic cup competition and had been out of the top four places all season **(BAD)**, but they pushed on at the end of the season and finished third **(GOOD)**.

The following years followed a similar pattern, with good and bad moments, rather than a critical succession of failures. When the anger of the fans was starting to boil over, they won two consecutive FA Cups, and in 2016 they were close to the top of the Premier League, but the title was to go instead to Leicester City.

There was a similar succession of instability in the 2016-2017 season. They didn't win either of their first two games in the Premier League **(BAD)**, but in October, after six consecutive victories, they were joint top of the league alongside Manchester City and Liverpool **(GOOD)**. Of the five league games they played between January 31 and March 18, they lost four. Between beating Hull City on February 11 and their next Premier League victory on April 5 against West Ham United, Arsenal only managed FA Cup wins against Sutton United and Lincoln City, teams from the fifth tier of English football. Bayern Munich thrashed them 5-1 in both legs of the Champions League last sixteen for an embarrassing aggregate 10-2 **(TERRIBLE)**.

But then Wenger changed to playing with a back three, a tactical switch that provided a certain amount of stability for the team, and Arsenal won nine of the last ten games of the season, including the FA Cup semi-final and final **(GOOD)**. However, they finished outside the top four and missed out on Champions League qualification **(BAD)**.

With the new TV contract coming into force in the Premier League, not qualifying for the Champions League is somewhat offset from a financial point of view—although it does still have an impact—and the board decided to offer him a new two-year contract, based more on the end of the season than an overall assessment of his last three-year cycle. Or indeed, without going so far back, an overall assessment of the season just finished, which was the first for twenty years where Arsenal didn't occupy one of the top four places in the Premier League.

As well as his questionable tactical decisions, Arsène Wenger's greatest stubbornness lies in not realizing that just after winning the 2017 FA Cup was the perfect time to go. But his ego is perhaps even bigger than Mourinho's. He does not want to leave without winning the Premier League again and doing it without spending the amount of money Manchester City, United, Chelsea, and co. spend. He's like a dog that is so obsessed with chasing its toy that it doesn't notice that there might be a motorway full of speeding cars or a gaping chasm ahead. But if Arsène Wenger were interested in seeing Arsenal winning an important trophy other than the FA Cup without worrying about who was sitting on the bench, he would already have allowed a fresh mind to have taken over the side. But no, Wenger puts his own personal blind ambition above the club's interests, which is really disastrous.

Faced with the possibility of Arsène Wenger's contract being renewed, the Arsenal Supporters' Trust carried out a survey in March 2017, and 78 percent of its members didn't support his continuing. To the question of whether they believed the way the board had dealt with Wenger's contract had been with the club's best interests at heart, 86 percent answered "NO."[15]

Although in practice that Premier League title may be achievable, he could only do it with a mentally strong squad and with players who play at a consistent level and who avoid injuries; these are things which Arsenal doesn't have. If Leicester City could do it in Claudio Ranieri's first season after spending the preceding year at the bottom of the table, why is it impossible for Arsenal? It's because they lack solidity, stability, and consistency.

There's nothing wrong with falling on your sword and removing yourself from the problem when you see that you can't find the solution. Football isn't an exact science, and psychological factors have a great influence. Sometimes, no matter how good you are, you can get confused and not find the right way ahead.

Wenger was the "solution" for Arsenal for a long time—the years with trophies and some without—but he's never accepted that winning the league again is not only down to him and that he can't remain in the post just in order to do it.

That's become something more than an objective for him; it's become an obsession. Arsène Wenger doesn't want to leave without winning the title again because he thinks that if he managed to do so it would be one in the eye for everyone who has criticized him since the Invincibles' run ended at Old Trafford in fall 2004.

And he's right, it certainly would be. He would leave glorious and triumphant. But what if he doesn't manage it? What price has he made the club pay to satisfy his craving? At what point does he finally stop trying?

The state of disrepair into which Arsenal has fallen is truly deplorable, and they have now lost their exclusive right to qualification for the Champions League, which previously had been guaranteed year after year.

The taunts of "Wenger out" have sprung up all over the world and even appear at music concerts now, making Arsenal a laughing stock. Keeping Wenger in post for so long hasn't only led to the team getting weaker, but it has also severely damaged the image of the club. If he really cared about the club, he would have left to avoid greater barbarity. But he only thinks of himself, and he doesn't see something which should be obvious for someone who—as he points out himself—has been in this business for over thirty years.

Wenger didn't tire of criticizing the fans for the constant displays of disaffection toward the team and defended himself against the campaigns against him with untruths, diverting the real meaning of the situation. He never seems to notice (at least publicly) that the complaints and that hostile atmosphere have always been directed at him and the directors, never at the players or at the club itself. The placards very clearly said "Wenger Out," not "Alexis Out," "Özil Out," or "Arsenal Out."

Someone who did quickly see when the right moment had come to move on and whose decision was vital for an upturn in his personal fortunes and those of his team was Jürgen Klopp. He's an example of personal maturity, humility, and real concern for Borussia Dortmund, the club he was a part of for seven years.

Dortmund hit an unexpected slump in the 2014-2015 season. At the winter break they were bottom of the league and an unimaginable debacle was on the cards. They had "given" Mario Götze and Robert Lewandowski to Bayern Munich, injuries had disrupted the squad, and the forwards signed in the summer, Ciro Immobile and Adrián Ramos, hadn't found their feet.

It was then that Klopp realized that he was no longer the person best equipped to continue to lead the Westfalenstadion club. "If I am not able to do something better than this, then I should not be here," was his level-headed assessment of the situation and his position there. When the manager has lost the ability to recover the hunger of his players, the best thing to do is to leave.

For some reason, which can in a way be attributed to the actual dynamic that drives the atmosphere of the dressing room and feeds a team's performances on the pitch, the Borussia Dortmund squad had lost the ability to motivate itself. They couldn't find a way to recover, and the defeats followed one after another. The defeats on the pitch created enormous psychological wounds.

The club was affected by many factors in a very short period of time. The endless injuries of its key men, several of its most important players leaving for their biggest rivals in the Bundesliga and the cloud of pessimism that brought with it, as well as the inevitable amount of luck that can sometimes bring a good team to its knees overnight, as it did with Mourinho's Chelsea after they won the league in 2015.

The change of manager was therefore imperative; all the players would do their best to impress the new person. With Klopp, some bad habits had been formed, and a new face was needed which everyone would want to seduce in order to be regular starters.

Thomas Tuchel, his carefully selected successor, promised stability and ambition of the type that had allowed Klopp to win the Bundesliga twice and reach the Champions League final. This was backed up by his results at Mainz, which was, coincidentally, the same club that had forged Klopp.

In his two seasons at the club, Tuchel returned Dortmund to the Champions League. In his first season, they took Bayern to the penultimate game of the season in their struggle for the Bundesliga title, and in his second season they won the German Cup. His departure came about because of differences with the board, and it had nothing to do with his management of the team.

Tuchel rescued the essence of Klopp's Dortmund and made it very clear that his work would have to be based on what his predecessor had built. Changing everything might have brought tragic consequences and wasn't the best way to win the players over. Klopp's legacy had to remain well beyond his departure, and the new manager decided to show how much could be gained from the style of play and the dynamic created by the man who now manages Liverpool.

But what did Tuchel do to rescue this giant from the bad times it was going through? He didn't need a magic wand or make drastic changes. He used a pinch of common sense, steadfast principles, and, especially, a lot of motivation.

He exploited the speed of his forwards to encourage long diagonal balls and balls played into the spaces. Dortmund doesn't play statically, but rather with endless movement of its players, who most of the time are on the attack.

It's the same modus operandi which took Klopp's Dortmund to glory and another good example of how to play very attacking football and how to defend with attackers. The emergence of Pierre-Emerick Aubameyang as a great potential goal-scorer—like Cristiano Ronaldo, without being a center forward—was key to the side's rebirth.

The success of this formation is based on using spaces and speed. It's very difficult to control a team when Marco Reus, Henrikh Mkhitaryan, Ousmane Dembélé, or Aubameyang start running and wait for a through ball from Ilkay Gündoğan, Shinji Kagawa, or Gonzalo Castro, or from each other.

Dortmund started to defend a little higher up the pitch, pressing the opposition when they got the ball back. The center backs started to move consistently up into the middle of the pitch to quickly cut out balls played to the opponents' center forward when the opposition team tried to beat the first pressing lines with a long ball to their most advanced player. The Dortmund forwards are very effective in immediately recovering the ball very high up the pitch so the center backs were able to complete their task very efficiently.

If Tuchel hadn't tried to do this, the team would have been very exposed because it normally attacks with six or seven men. As the referees in the Bundesliga don't show too many cards, the defenders can afford themselves the luxury of committing a lot of fouls; this is mitigated by the fact that the majority are committed in midfield, when the opposition hasn't yet put together a properly organized attack.

Forwards contributing to defensive duties is something that Tuchel brought back to perfection. With Borussia Dortmund, fluency takes precedence over everything else; players don't stop running, and dynamism is king.

But in order for the players to buy into the need to be running for every one of the 5,400 seconds a match lasts, you need to have great motivational powers. You need to be able to convey your idea and for your players to implement it not because it's what the manager has told them to do, but because they are completely convinced that it's the best thing for them and for everyone as a team.

Thomas Tuchel showed that the potential of that Dortmund was just lying dormant and hadn't actually died in Jürgen Klopp's last season. And although important players like Mario Götze, Robert Lewandowski, and then Hummels, Mkhitaryan, and Gündoğan had left, and others had left and then returned, like Kagawa and Nuri Şahin, good replacements had come in, such as Castro, Guerreiro, Bartra, and Dembélé.

The post-Lewandowski pairing of Adrián Ramos and Ciro Immobile didn't work, and that was to be expected. Although both attackers have some characteristics in common with the Pole—Ramos is good in the air and Immobile is very fast—Lewandowski, as the great player he is, has them all. Apart from that, neither of the two was able to overcome the hurdle of adapting to a new club. So something had to change.

Although often a player's second season is better than his first—Henry at Barça—Tuchel preferred to change the model and to attack without a natural number 9. He realized that speed, the ability to get away from their marker, and the finishing prowess of Reus, Aubameyang, Dembélé, and Mkhitaryan (before his departure for Manchester United) could allow them to create enough chances and score enough goals. Everyone was orchestrated using a formation which could change its men and its configuration from the midfield forward, but which never modified the way it functioned.

The presence of Gonzalo Castro, just as Koke does at Atlético de Madrid, offers that flexibility to be able to play close to the holding midfielder or farther up the pitch as an advanced midfielder.

Tuchel went for an approach which, without Lewandowski, got the best out of the rest of his players, and he wasn't afraid of setting up with four clearly defined attackers.

Perhaps no sentence in the history of football contains a greater truth than the one spoken by Guardiola when he was asked for the secret of that Barça side that steamrollered everything in its path: "*I just ask my players not to stop running*." That's what the Dortmund players do, and that was the result in the post-Klopp era.

Another of the fantastic consequences of Tuchel's system was the way he exploits opponents' mistakes. You need to bring the ball out in a very meticulous and well-structured fashion to not succumb to those black and yellow lions who pounce on their opponents when they lose possession. They create chaos and make the most of it.

To do this, it's essential that the forwards press. Dortmund knows that its opponents will make a mistake several times every game and that an apparently adverse situation could lead to a clear goal-scoring opportunity. When their opponents think they have mounted a counterattack, an unexpected turnover triggers a devastating attack the other way.

The Borussia Dortmund midfield is a transitional area. They don't need an N'Golo Kanté type of holding midfielder because everyone takes every step necessary to recover the ball, even if that means that forwards have to track back to their own area to do so, although Julian Weigl does provide the calm authority required to take the ball from the center backs and move it forward to the side's attacking block.

However, Tuchel had nothing against possession. Dortmund pressing after losing the ball suggests that without it they are nothing. However, they don't play with a long series of passes, but with a more direct, front-on style, aware of the implicit risk of verticality but promoting the unquestionable benefits of one-touch football.

Tuchel discovered that Aubameyang has the capacity to get into the area as the attacking spearhead because of his pace, his finishing ability, and his unpredictability. There's no reason for him to be restricted to just being an orchestrator/assist provider so that another center forward, like Lewandowski before, should shoulder more of the goal-scoring responsibility. That was perhaps one of his best decisions, because Aubameyang responded like one of the most lethal forwards in Europe, scoring seventy-nine goals in the two seasons he played under Thomas Tuchel.

Playing Aubameyang on the periphery for periods doesn't bother him; he doesn't need to be rooted to the penalty area because one of his most dangerous weapons is the runs he makes from deeper when least expected. He's also backed up by other forwards, who move into more central and advanced positions when he moves out wide or drops back.

In the Bundesliga, only Bayern Munich have the reliable antidote for this virus, and that's why Borussia Dortmund, not just with Tuchel but with Jürgen Klopp before him, scored so many goals after winning the ball back in the final third of the pitch.

Tuchel's departure left the spectacular work he had done in his two years at the Westfalenstadion unfinished. While in his second season they let Bayern and Leipzig get away in the race for the league title early on, they reached the Champions League quarter-final and won the German Cup. The team recovered from the dip in Jürgen Klopp's last season all because of Klopp's good sense and judgement in realizing that it was time to leave and the fantastic job Thomas Tuchel did when he took over, keeping what deserved to be kept and changing what needed to be changed. The arrival of a manager often saves a club; sometimes, so does a manager making the decision to leave.

Chapter 4

THE FORMATION, FLOURISHING, AND ECLIPSE OF THE MANCHESTER CITY MIDFIELD—GUARDIOLA'S INHERITANCE

In order to understand the evolution of the Manchester City midfield in recent years, we need to go back to the very origins of these changes, with the arrival of Roberto Mancini in December 2009.

Despite the Italian's time at the Etihad Stadium providing that last-minute Premier League title win and the team acquiring a style of play which has lasted until today, it was a fairly tortuous process getting there, particularly because of the way Mancini chose to set up his most frequent starting eleven.

Although Manchester City had one of the most potent attacks in the league, Mancini was quite conservative at first, and he adopted a crazy idea that in time would become an astute tactical option. In spite of the plethora of good forwards in the squad, such as Carlos Tévez, Emmanuel Adebayor, Roque Santa Cruz, David Silva, Shaun Wright-Phillips, Adam Johnson, and James Milner, the team started to be identified by the hyper-population of its midfield.

Mancini started playing with Tévez as a lone forward and Nigel de Jong, Gareth Barry, and Yaya Touré in midfield, which could be seen as somewhat unnecessary, illogical, and counterproductive. What need is there to have these three players on the pitch when two of them, in any combination, are perfectly capable of providing a solid and functional midfield?

That was when Touré started playing in the number 10 position which he would later fill with unquestionable skill but which he found very difficult to get used to at first.

The Ivory Coast player felt somewhat lost on the pitch and City played boring, clumsy football and looked like an alien team in the Premier League. It was as if Mancini wanted a number 10 come what may, but instead of using the club's vast resources to sign a player who was a natural in the position, he decided to transform a player who was brilliant, but in other aspects of the game.

That 4–3–2–1, which was fairly similar to certain Italian footballing principles, didn't seem the best choice, but even so Mancini made it his most frequently used formation.

However, on the day when he decided to try something different, a 4–4–2 with Touré and Barry in midfield, Silva and Milner as advanced midfielders, and Adebayor and Balotelli up front, they lost 1-2 away at Wolverhampton Wanderers at the end of October 2010.

The strangest thing about this game was when City was behind, Mancini took off Adebayor, put Pablo Zabaleta on, and moved Yaya Touré forward to a number 10 position. Taking a forward off and putting a defender on to play in midfield was a strange way to get back into the game, but at least he was faithful to his principles. Mancini had a theory to prove and was determined to defend his own beliefs.

Perhaps he would say that fate is a cruel mistress. While one game shouldn't be used as a reference, the starting lineup for this game was much more sensible than the one Mancini usually opted for, but it wasn't something his players were used to. This defeat removed any thoughts of sticking to the system, and for the next game, away to West Brom, he returned to his usual central triumvirate.

Before that insipid defeat against Wolves, Manchester City had lost 0-3 at home against Arsenal after Dedryck Boyata's red card five minutes in. The team was left with ten men and was hyper-exposed, without weapons or anything else to cling on to. As the home team, they might have been expected to have achieved something not quite so poor in terms of quality and to have put up a show which wasn't so bereft of fight, but this was something which hadn't been impregnated in the team's DNA.

Against Manchester United, also at home, something similar happened. As expected, Mancini used the predicted 4–3–2–1 system, and Yaya Touré was given the duty of directing the play and distributing the ball in the forward areas of the midfield, as well as getting into the box on other occasions to get shots in like a center forward.

He didn't perform any of these functions well, and City's approach centered around breaking down United's play, which stopped them from having a shred of fluency themselves. They were just like the proverbial dog in a manger, neither eating nor allowing anyone else to eat. The result was a dull, goalless draw.

The following week, also at the Etihad Stadium, this time against Birmingham City, what Mancini did was even more incomprehensible. He started the game with only two players in the defensive area of the midfield, de Jong and Touré, and played three attacking midfielders, Silva, Milner and Adam Johnson, and as usual, Carlos Tévez started as the lone striker.

After sixty-six minutes, with the score still 0-0, he decided to be a little more positive in his search for all three points. He took James Milner off and put Roque Santa Cruz on, one of the very rare moments that season, which we could count on the fingers of one hand, where he had two forwards on the pitch.

But that day Mancini was not going to change. He continued to be a manager searching hurriedly and erratically for an effective style of football, yet using a formation that was lacking in sense, and after eighty-three minutes he replaced Carlos Tévez with Gareth Barry.

The only reference point for the attack was then the Paraguayan Santa Cruz, who hadn't played for a long time and for whom this was the only appearance in a City shirt in the whole first half of the season before going to Blackburn Rovers on loan in January. It goes without saying that the score didn't change.

Between December and January 1, they won five games out of six, only losing 1-2 at home against an Everton side which played for half an hour with ten men, but on January 5 against Arsenal at the Emirates Stadium, Mancini did something inexplicable again.

In the three previous games, all of which they won, against Newcastle, Aston Villa, and Blackpool, the Italian manager used his usual three central midfielders and one lone striker. But now, against Arsenal, a team that dominates possession and against whom it makes a little more sense to bolster the midfield, he not only used two center forwards, but Tévez's companion was Jô, a man who barely played the whole season.

That was the perfect day not to have played him, as he needed forwards who helped out consistently and skillfully with defensive duties; attacks were going to have to be organized around recovering the ball very close to their own area and by linking all their players through a gradual progression up the pitch. That afternoon, Manchester City needed to be very precise and energetic with the tactics employed, and only a very structured approach would allow them to achieve victory. What was the sense, then, in depending on an out-of-form player with suspect goal-scoring ability and little talent for defensive duties?

Jô played for sixty-five minutes, went about unnoticed, and ended up being replaced by Adam Johnson, who in most people's eyes would have made a better choice as a starter. That day, all Manchester City did was defend, and they showed that Roberto Mancini's priority was first to protect his own goal and then try to attack however he could, without a clear desire to play attacking football in the first place.

Indeed, Mancini himself acknowledged as much after drawing away against Birmingham City one month later.

> *I like 1-0 wins. When you don't concede a goal and you have players like Edin Džeko, Carlos Tévez or David Silva, you win 90 per cent. I prefer we are boring for two to three matches and we win 1-0. If you watch teams that won titles, they conceded very few goals.*[16]

In January, Edin Džeko arrived from Wolfsburg and revealed another contradiction in the Italian manager. From then on, he consistently started with two center forwards—Džeko and Tévez—which makes you wonder why he hadn't done so before when he had Emmanuel Adebayor, Mario Balotelli, Roque Santa Cruz, and Jô himself in the squad. So what was the problem, the model or the players? If Mancini thought the most coherent thing was to play with two clearly defined forwards, why didn't he do everything possible to adopt this system with the long list of forwards he already had?

Although Manchester City more frequently lined up with two forwards in that second half of the 2010-2011 season, Mancini still chose to use Yaya Touré as the third man in midfield in a role that was quite similar to that of a playmaker. At times he also clung to crazy ideas like using Pablo Zabaleta as a midfielder or Aleksandar Kolarov as a winger, despite the fact that he had a squad full of players for whom these were natural positions.

However, Manchester City defeated Manchester United in the FA Cup semi-final because of Michael Carrick's stupid mistake and Paul Scholes' no less infantile red card. In the final, Stoke City presented no clear threat, and although the game was still goalless until its last few minutes, Yaya Touré became the goal-scoring hero again and paved the way to the trophy. Needless to say, in both games Mancini started with Barry, de Jong, and Touré in midfield, with the Ivory Coast player in his new role as the number 10.

Despite all the money spent on new players, this team had a squad which could have been fighting for the Premier League title, but they had to be content with snatching the fourth spot from Spurs—exactly the opposite of what had happened the previous season.

The FA Cup and Champions League qualification wasn't a bad quantitative outcome, but that season highlighted Roberto Mancini's fears, his panic about using a sensible lineup, his poor feel for fluid football, his obvious stubbornness in continuing to opt for an irrational formation, and the shifting of Yaya Touré to a completely unknown function.

Mancini's fears were laid bare again in the Community Shield in August 2011 against the Premier League champions Manchester United. He started with a 4–4–2 with Yaya Touré together with Nigel de Jong in the defensive midfield area, and they went up 2-0, but United reacted after half-time and quickly drew level.

One minute after conceding the equalizer, Mancini took Mario Balotelli off and put Gareth Barry on in his place. However much Yaya Touré was moved forward, why would you tactically capitulate like that? Why would you give your opponent a chance to feel more comfortable? Why would you give up the opportunity to fight on an equal footing for a trophy that is decided by a one-off game? What image are you giving your players, your fans, and the watching world?

As might have been expected, after that, Manchester City adopted a completely timid approach, was unable to create the slightest danger, and dedicated itself entirely to defending. Fate was fair with Roberto Mancini, since in added time Vincent Kompany committed a defensive howler as the last man, allowing Nani to run through unopposed, and Manchester United lifted the trophy.

However, it seems that the warning bell was heeded, and Mancini started to alter his starting formations. The arrival of Kun Agüero and Samir Nasri meant a reduction in the frequency with which he used the tactical formation that had been his flagship in the previous season, the 4–3–2–1, and he started to opt for a more "natural" starting eleven, although the tactical alternative he turned to most in times of need was to add a third holding midfielder and move Yaya Touré forward to play as a number 10.

For example, in the Champions League group phase against Bayern Munich, when they were losing 0-2, he tried unsuccessfully to rescue the game like that.

In the next European match against Villarreal he was even more radical. After forty minutes and down by one goal, he sacrificed Adam Johnson, sending Gareth Barry on and moving Yaya Touré forward. It was as if that was the formation that made Mancini feel most secure, and he was infatuated with the idea of making it work whatever the consequences.

Soon after that change, there was a spectacular Manchester City move which ended up forcing Villarreal to put through their own net. Later, Agüero, who came on in the second half for Nigel de Jong in an attempt to return to the initial 4–4–2, scored a last-gasp winner.

Manchester City was becoming a solid, balanced side and was starting to acquire a very clear identity: The midfield was the team's guide, the kitchen where attacking football was prepared and gave the squad a clear, dependable reference point to hold on to. David Silva was its master in chief, fast, unpredictable, and with a great talent for creating goal-scoring opportunities.

City started to be the most convincing force in the Premier League, defeating Manchester United 6-1 at Old Trafford and remaining unbeaten in the Premier League since the start of the season until they lost away to Chelsea on December 12 after playing more than half of the second half with ten men.

The handbrake effect of using three central midfielders was evident with the use of James Milner, a player who lost his duties as a winger when he went to Manchester City and became a more central footballer. Although the previous season Mancini had used Milner more in balancing than attacking duties, he now held him back a little less and gave him greater freedom on the right wing, although he always required him to be present when City moved into defensive mode.

But a leopard doesn't change its spots. After their Champions League elimination in the group phase of the 2011-2012 season, the Europa League draw dealt City a very hard two-legged tie against Porto, the reigning champions of the tournament who had also dropped out of the Champions League.

Mancini became the same fearful person as before and again played Gareth Barry and Nigel de Jong, together with Yaya Touré, who was free to play as a number 10 and who would also occasionally pop up as a number 9.

When Manchester City lost the ball, Touré would retreat to the base of the midfield and become another defender. His priority was to contain his opponent regardless of whether the team was effective going forward or not.

Although they won the game 2-1, both goals came from two crass Porto mistakes rather than being crafted by City's players. Despite having strengthened the defense of his midfield, Mancini didn't manage to stem the tide of attacks from the Portuguese side, who frankly played much better on the night.

It's incredible that for the whole season Mancini had used a tactical approach that had worked in the vast majority of matches, but he now decided to opt for its antithesis, the very same approach that had brought him so many doubts the season before.

The stability of a midfield that had acquired a shape and a style was therefore rocked, and it now became unsure of itself with so many sudden tactical changes.

They lost their Premier League lead at Swansea, where he started with Yaya Touré as number 10, but after thirty-seven minutes, with the game still scoreless, decided to change it all around by replacing Gareth Barry with Kun Agüero because City hadn't been able to create anything at all. How could he possibly give so little time to the starting lineup he considered to be the right one for the game? Was it really the right one?

Against Chelsea at home he started with 4–4–2, but after the break, with the game at 0-0, he made his "magical change" and moved Yaya Touré to play as number 10. In the second half they conceded an unfortunate goal and went back to 4–4–2 with Tévez coming on for Nigel de Jong. His changes were clearly not a response to a sober analysis of the situation, but were the fruit of desperate, even random, decisions.

It seems very strange that away at Stoke City, one of the hardest places to play in England, Mancini did something completely new which went against his tactical approach up to then. Manchester City were down 0-1 down, but he never moved Yaya Touré up to his number 10 position; instead, he left him back as his only holding midfielder. Would you believe it!

Football is so unpredictable that it was Yaya Touré himself who got the draw with a very powerful shot from over thirty meters (100 feet) which took a deflection off Ryan Shawcross just in front of the goalkeeper.

In the last games of that 2011-2012 season, Mancini lost a bit of confidence in David Silva, and although he didn't remove him from the starting lineup, he did often substitute him in the second half.

Around then, Manchester United let an eight-point lead slip in just two weeks when they lost the key derby match against Manchester City. On that night, Mancini again took a forward off, put a holding midfielder on, and moved Yaya Touré up to his number 10 position in the second half when City were ahead 1-0. The team didn't lose its solidity and ended up securing the victory that took them back to the top of the league.

The following week they had a very difficult game against Alan Pardew's surprising Newcastle side, who finished fifth in the league. When he saw that the 4–4–2 he'd started with wasn't working, Mancini took Carlos Tévez off, replacing him with Nigel de Jong and letting Yaya Touré roam around the fringes of the opposition's penalty area. Two goals from the Ivorian left Manchester City within touching distance of the league title, which they would win on the last day with Kun Agüero's last-gasp goal against Queens Park Rangers.

Roberto Mancini ended up showing that there was a grain of truth in his stubborn theory that Yaya Touré could play successfully away from his designated position of holding midfielder. How he discovered this is still a mystery, because Touré hadn't done this in any of his previous teams, and in his three seasons with Barça he had played as the most deep-lying midfielder.

It had taken hard work and some time, but Manchester City had become a team that welcomed possession of the ball as their most precious treasure and who had developed several ways to create goals, some as unorthodox as using Yaya Touré as the man to take on the titanic task of resolving stalemates. Mancini benefited from the power of his shots and his unstoppable drives forward in and around the area. Touré displayed an endless array of weapons that hadn't been seen before and was an effective alternative when the refined and subtle creativity of David Silva and Samir Nasri didn't bear fruit at any point.

That season did see a lot more sense from Mancini, as he didn't force through the implementation at all costs of a formation which the previous season hadn't produced the consistency to justify it always being used from the start. However, it could, and indeed did, become an occasional option to turn games around when City was in trouble.

Manchester City was acquiring a clearly defined identity and was on the right track, because despite the bumps they came across on the road, which are inevitable for any team, dominating possession of the ball will always be a swift and effective way of getting good results. If we add to this the owners' checkbook and Kun Agüero's excellent adaptation to the Premier League, this seed seemed to be germinating a strong and fruitful tree.

But in the 2012-2013 season, after winning the Premier League title, Mancini came up against an obstacle he had seen on certain occasions in the previous season. Manchester City's opponents defended as a block, and the team was often swallowed up in a long series of sideways passes on the edge of the area that didn't produce consistent goal-scoring opportunities.

This was so much the case that in the season before they scored ninety-three goals in the Premier League, but in that one they only scored sixty-six and were easily overtaken by Manchester United in terms of both goals and points. This can partly be explained by Mancini's tendency to be too tactically rigid and to worry too much about his team's response to losing the ball.

It's as if he had taken the creative phase of a dominant, abrasive midfield for granted, thinking that for City to get further in the Champions League and be even more "Barcelona-like" in their play he needed to iron out certain defensive issues.

That was when he placed more emphasis on the 11 against 0 training method. All 11 men from a theoretical Manchester City lineup would take up positions in one half of the pitch, and Mancini would be at the other end with a ball at his feet.

Then the manager would start to move toward random positions, trying to inculcate in his players the areas they had to cover according to where their opponents moved, something they had to repeat like robots.

This lack of freedom meant that the players lost the ability to improvise, which is basic in a sport as unpredictable as football, and the decrease in the number of goals the team scored was an inevitable result.

The way he seized on the 11 against 0 is a clue that he was starting to worry more about defensive organization, perhaps thinking that his forwards would continue to find a way to score the same number of goals, but that the dominance Manchester City managed to exert in terms of possession, which in turn is an indicator of the global dominance of a game, would not be affected.

But no season is the same as another, and what works perfectly today may not do so tomorrow. Mistakes with marking led Manchester City to let in key goals, despite Mancini focusing so much on avoiding it. He also sometimes went with a false 3–5–2 with Aleksandar Kolarov as the fifth free player on the left wing, but that didn't work very well either.

Roberto Mancini continued to play Yaya Touré as a number 10 in certain games, but without a logical pattern that might help to understand an occasional tactical need for it. He did it, for example, against Real Madrid and Ajax in the group phase of the Champions League, two potentially difficult games, against Chelsea in the Premier League, and also in apparently easier games against Reading or in both Wigan games. In the vast majority of the games where he played the Ivorian as a number 10 he didn't get a positive result and ended up returning to an orthodox 4–4–2, when City did score, rescue points, and, often, win.

The number of occasions in which Mancini started games with two holding midfielders and then changed formation to push Yaya Touré forward to the "magical" position decreased. He actually did it in four games, and the final result was never better than the score at the time of his changing the formation.

Counting against that option was the fact that Touré clashed positionally with Samir Nasri and David Silva on the edge of the area when Manchester City was trying to find a way through the iron wall erected by their opponents. Mancini had made the use of these two playmakers the norm, and they had become very dominant when it came to taking on the creative duties. You can have two players like that on the pitch, but if you add a third one, then one of them will lose their protagonism. In this case, it was Yaya Touré who lost out.

The opponents learned what the best way was to defend against City and were doing so well at it that Mancini was left reeling at his inability to rediscover the lost goal-scoring effectiveness of his team. He was becoming a kind of new tinker man, as there was no end in sight for his changes in tactics and players.

Indeed, in that game away to Ajax, which City ended up losing 3-1, he finished with four forwards on the pitch—Tévez, Džeko, Agüero, and Balotelli—a clear symptom not only of his irascible despair, but also of his lack of tactical acumen.

Against Liverpool and Southampton in February 2013, Mancini showed that he didn't have things clear in his own mind. He changed formation several times during those games, playing with an improvised three-man defense at times, but never using Yaya Touré at the top of the midfield triangle.

That season, far from being the further development of an idea that had bloomed the previous season, got stuck in the mire of Mancini's obsession with making certain players play in completely new positions, his excessive concern for defensive solidity, and even the poor form of some of his players. The team was so consumed with trying to understand his formations that they were caught up in his own web.

Yaya Touré wasn't as effective as a "10" at the start of games, and he was used very little in that role to try to turn a game around when City was behind.

Mancini left after falling victim to his own mistakes, because he was largely responsible for the critical imbalance in Manchester City that season. But no team is immune to flaws, and even the best managers in the world find themselves in certain situations they find difficult to resolve. Football is also a matter of trial and error at times. His sacking, just twelve months after signing a five-year contract extension, was fairly deplorable. It's not easy now to find a good manager, and if we add the large dose of uncertainty which is inherent in the sport, we understand that one bad season is very little time in which to reach such drastic conclusions.

The Mancini era had its footballing highs and lows, something no team can escape, but if he did things ostensibly wrong when he arrived, over time he came to convert City into a dominant side which could easily be set back on a winning course because it had a clearly defined, solid identity with the most influential midfield in the whole Premier League.

What happened to Mancini was similar to what would happen three years later to his successor, Manuel Pellegrini. For months, the English press had been reporting that the Chilean would be replacing him, and Mancini lost his temper after losing the FA Cup final to Wigan and publicly called the club's press department into question for not having put an end to the rumors.

The relationship between the Italian and the club's directors, which was already shaky, was now fractured, and two days later his sacking was announced.

However, how is the next manager to accept the challenge going to feel if he knows that only short-term success will save his neck? Does it make sense to force someone to work under such pressure?

Even Sir Alex Ferguson came out against Mancini leaving, and he repeated his feelings a few years later in his book *Leading*: "*There is no evidence that constantly sacking managers gives you better results*."[17]

Another one of the reasons given in the statement announcing his departure was that Mancini, despite having guided the club to its first league title in forty-four years, hadn't paid enough attention to working on the reserve squad. What a contradiction! Was the sheikhs' idea really to buy a team, buy directors, copy other models, and buy football itself in order to then try and rebuild it? Where is the border between buying and rebuilding to be found?

The best thing an owner can do is carefully select a manager and trust him, always bearing in mind the possibility that results might vary within a given range and not necessarily be what was expected. There are clubs that have had good seasons and then one bad one, and they've managed to recover again with the same manager. The best example is Sir Alex Ferguson at Manchester United: He didn't win the Premier League or the Champions League every season, but in the twenty-six years he was at Old Trafford, nobody won more than him.

What would have happened if Ferguson had been sacked after three seasons without winning the Premier League between 2004 and 2006? Would United have won three consecutive league titles and the League–

Champions League double in 2008? Up to now, four years after his departure, Manchester United hasn't been league or Champions League winners with three different managers.

All common sense around the work of managers has disappeared with the growing need for immediate success instilled by the oligarch owners, who have little knowledge of football and who are only interested in trophies as a way to be economically profitable. This even happens in clubs that have presidents rather than owners, such as Real Madrid.

The press has a lot to do with this, and society itself has been molded by this increasing aura of "now or never" which the media drip-feeds. People end up being convinced that a bad run—sometimes not even a bad season—is enough reason to get sacked, and that same feeling is transmitted to the clubs' owners. If there were more claims against unfair dismissal, like that of Carlo Ancelotti at Real Madrid, Tata Martino at Barça, and even David Moyes at Manchester United, perhaps the owners would feel more restricted when making such drastic decisions with so little justification. But the world is convinced that there's no tomorrow and that it's all right to sack a manager if he goes ten games without a win.

We may well wonder whether Manchester City would have sacked their manager if it wasn't Pep Guardiola who lost 4-0 at Everton in his first season, falling to fifth place in the Premier League, ten points behind the leader. Guardiola was probably the only manager in the world who was, at that point, able to survive a situation like that.

Managers all have similar pressure when they lead a team, and sometimes they choose clubs where they sign up to be sacked the day they sign their contracts. There is obviously a keen desire to work and not to have their careers cut short, but such haste is the perfect complement in creating this unstoppable whirlwind of new contracts and sackings afflicting today's game. There's no calm, no peace, either from the position of the managers choosing a club, or from the owners giving them the necessary time and space in which to work. The manager is always the weakest point in the chain, and it's becoming a more and more fragile position.

MANUEL PELLEGRINI— PLAN A MANAGER

Although Manchester City lost four Premier League games in the first three months of the 2013-2014 season, they were clearly the team best equipped to win the league and had the most solid and coherent approach throughout the campaign.

They showed that the strength of the midfield built by Mancini was destined to last if the players were given the freedom to play without so many tactical chains. Pellegrini arrived, watered the plant, watched it bloom again in a matter of days, and squeezed every last drop of power from Yaya Touré to the point where he scored twenty-four goals in all competitions that season, twenty of which came in the Premier League.

The Chilean didn't change the basic principles of the team, kept Silva as the creative axis while Samir Nasri, Jesús Navas, and James Milner took turns in the other attacking midfield position, and the arrival of Fernandinho offered a double tank of oxygen.

Navas arrived to offer pace on the right side and a great ability to stretch the pitch, which were things that no other player in the squad could offer at that time. In his first months in charge, Pellegrini regularly kept two players up front, almost always Kun Agüero and Álvaro Negredo.

In one of those four defeats, against Chelsea on October 27, Pellegrini used Yaya Touré in the number 10 position for the first time. Behind, offering him protection, were Javi García and Fernandinho.

But he came up against what had sometimes happened to Mancini the previous season: Silva and Nasri took on the creation in the last third of the pitch while Yaya Touré wandered desperately around that area without being able to exert a clear influence on the *playmaking*.

At Southampton something similar happened. They were being dominated by Mauricio Pochettino's side and had very few goal-scoring opportunities. Pellegrini then took Negredo off, put Javi García on, and moved Yaya Touré forward to the "magical" position, but the presence of Nasri, and to some degree the situation in the game, stopped the Ivorian from taking on a leading role in Manchester City's offensive play.

The second game against Chelsea, at home on Monday, February 3, which became famous for Mourinho's master plan for victory, was the first evidence that Manuel Pellegrini wasn't able to find an effective solution to a particular situation that was completely out of the ordinary.

City suffered the loss of two key players, Kun Agüero and Fernandinho. Edin Džeko isn't a striker who finds himself heavily involved in the build-up play, doesn't have the same pace to be able to find spaces, and doesn't have the same refined finishing ability as the Argentinian.

Fernandinho was better suited to defending, allowing City to do so with fewer players and thus be more lethal both with slow build-ups and swift counterattacks. Without him, the side found it difficult to start a clean and tidy attacking transition.

To make matters worse, the player Pellegrini was forced to replace him with that day, Martín Demichelis, had lost the ability to play in that position, and he contributed absolutely nothing to the game. They set out to defend the same as they always did and were completely exposed by a wise, cold, and calculating Chelsea.

Pellegrini was unable to find a coherent plan to cover the absence of both players. For example, when the team lost the ball, David Silva didn't get back enough to help with the initial creation of the attacks, and Yaya Touré wasn't close enough to Demichelis to avoid leaving him at the mercy of the opposition forwards, especially bearing in mind that the Argentinian was booked after thirty-seven minutes.

Pellegrini was also unable to change his formation as the match wore on to avoid being punished by Chelsea's approach. He should have employed a form of attack which fitted with the ability to defend well, responding to how Mourinho's side were attacking. City gave Ramires, Willian and Hazard a lot of space between the midfield and their defense and didn't concern themselves with deciphering the enigma, "*First I analyze how I must defend and then I will know how I have to attack.*"

That day showed that Fernandinho was essential in the difficult matches, indeed that the real lethal weapon was his duo with Yaya Touré, because the sum of the two players was greater than the isolated value of their parts.

It was the first time that season that Manchester City had been so ineffective as an attacking threat, due to the absence of a plan B and two of their most important players.

Mourinho knew how to cope with his deficiencies, but Pellegrini couldn't get it right when it came to smoothing over the cracks left by his missing players, even though City was much more consistent over the season than Chelsea when they weren't in unusual situations.

Five days later—still without Agüero and Fernandinho—Manchester City traveled to Norwich, and Manuel Pellegrini didn't repeat his mistake of playing Demichelis together with Yaya Touré or the two center forwards

Džeko and Negredo, who are very much alike and don't have a great deal of talent for playing outside the area. You often need your number 9 not only to be an infallible goal-scorer, but also to come away from their comfort zone and work with the teammates around them when needed.

Now James Milner was Yaya Touré's partner in midfield, and Stevan Jovetić, a much more mobile playmaker, joined Negredo in attack. But they came up against a Norwich City side which was very well organized defensively, closing down all the spaces around the edge of the area and causing a few frights in isolated forays on Joe Hart's goal. Jesús Navas couldn't make progress on the right wing, and David Silva was also unable to find a pass that would give one of the forwards a clear sight of goal.

Fifteen minutes into the second half, Pellegrini decided to try something different. He took Jovetić off, put Džeko on in his place, and fifteen minutes later Negredo made way for Aleksandar Kolarov.

While having Džeko and Negredo on the pitch together may be considered counterproductive—which is debatable—and the second substitution may be questionable given the state of the game, the nature of the changes and the sudden adjustment of the formation are what show that Pellegrini wasn't able to cope with the situation he'd been presented with and wasn't equipped to get the right results when two of his key players were missing.

It's true that with that same formation City may have won 0-3 if they had taken just 10 percent of the chances they created, but both the players and Pellegrini himself missed the starting lineup.

When the first bumps appeared in the road, as they will for any team, particularly in a league as competitive as the Premier League, Pellegrini showed that he didn't have the vision needed to see them coming or to find a solution once deficiencies had become apparent on the pitch. His decisions were desperate, and he looked unsure of himself.

The Chilean manager started to show signs that there was no master plan for the big games, and he just settled for allowing his players to do what they know best and to enjoy themselves on the pitch. That has to be the main weapon, of course, the one which must never be missing, but when your opponent doesn't do the same, you also need a bit of the Mourinho mentality.

A team aspiring to everything must be strong against strong opposition, and Manchester City had crumbled when they had come up against certain difficult obstacles. They looked weak under pressure and very ineffective when Yaya Touré and Fernandinho weren't together in midfield.

However, thanks to that slip by Steven Gerrard against Chelsea and with the help of the historic comeback by Crystal Palace on that wretched Monday for Liverpool, City ended up winning the Premier League by chance.

Deserved? The following seasons allowed us to see that it wasn't really.

The 2014-2015 season for Manchester City wasn't, in any way, a steady ride. Many were the flaws, the ups and downs, that presented themselves to an increasingly insecure team, although they still had a solid, functional midfield that believed in having possession of the ball as an axis for their existence.

Between October and November, they hit a bad patch when they only won one game in six—the derby against Manchester United; they lost at home to CSKA Moscow in the Champions League, to Newcastle in the League Cup, and to West Ham United in the Premier League. They also drew away to CSKA and QPR. The international break at that time turned out to be a saving grace for City.

After those two weeks of inactivity, they recovered quickly, to the point of securing nine straight wins; even when the injuries to Edin Džeko and Kun Agüero forced Manuel Pellegrini to play with no recognized forwards against Crystal Palace, they still managed to ease to a 3-0 victory.

This upturn in form was made possible by the solid foundations on which the team was built, and it was very unlikely to disappear for long. Quality possession of the ball was inculcated in the Mancini era, and it was enhanced by the consistency of the players who made up the Manchester City midfield at that time.

However, in January the car ran out of gas again. Five games without a win, knocked out of the FA Cup at home by the Championship side Middlesbrough, and with the last sixteen Champions League tie against Barcelona approaching.

Barça beat them again at the Etihad, just as they had the previous season, and Pellegrini displayed a certain naivety when he spoke after the first leg: "*If we played in the first half in the way we did the second, I think we would have done better*."[18]

What a discovery, and what a way to analyze his team's performance. If Manchester City was unable to play at the same level for the whole ninety minutes, that was entirely down to him and his players, and there was no external factor at play which stopped them. He even said that the players were unable to string three passes together in the first half, as if he were trying to shift all blame from his tactical approach and his team selection onto the players he sent out onto the pitch.

Once again it was clear that the Chilean manager doesn't have the dexterity needed to absorb the inevitable bumps in the road, and that the team functions well as long as plan A doesn't fall apart, or when very simple solutions are effective. But don't ask him for anything slightly more complex.

Manchester City finds it very difficult to play a decent match against one of Europe's big teams; they play in a highly demanding league, and they can't buy titles now—indeed, they had to pay for the right to compete for them. UEFA forced them to pay 60 million Euros (69 million dollars) at the start of the 2014-2015 season to enter the Champions League as a penalty for their huge debts and spending on players.

Vincent Kompany is an unsteady defender, particularly when he leaves his area and moves forward to midfield to break up an attack. But Pellegrini hasn't been able to build a defensive structure which will make this happen as little as possible.

City's attacking machine is their main strength, but introducing Yaya Touré or Fernandinho into that highly trustworthy attacking unit usually leaves them stretched at the back and exposes the weaknesses of a clumsy and vain Kompany.

At Chelsea, a very similar yet at the same time very different situation occurred. Around three years before, John Terry started to show signs that his shelf life as a central defender was coming to an end. But Mourinho, when he returned to Stamford Bridge, noticed that either because of the legend-like status that Terry had acquired at the club or because he could still exploit his permanent qualities as a stationary defender, he was able to build a solid defense with his captain as the flag-bearer.

To do this, he limited his forays outside the area and put a top player alongside him, Nemanja Matić. It was perhaps under Rafa Benítez that

Terry started to notice that once you reach the age of thirty you can no longer claim to have the recovery speed of a Raphaël Varane and that he was better becoming a pure box defender.

But as Benítez was just holding up the beams so the roof didn't fall in, we can't give him all the credit for Terry's resurrection. It was after Mourinho returned that his real rebirth took place, to the point that he played every minute in the Premier League in the season when Chelsea were proclaimed champions in 2015.

At Manchester City there was nobody who could play in the same position as Matić to cover the frailties of the center backs. There were two good central midfielders in Yaya Touré and Fernandinho, who lose nothing when compared to Matić, but the way they play doesn't offer protection for one of the team's weakest points.

However, Manchester City continued to show occasional evidence that their purest essence didn't stem from those two midfielders, although it was still hidden away in a little corner and sometimes difficult to get out. They needed to win away to Roma to stay alive in the Champions League—not easy at all—and they were forced to do so without Agüero, Yaya Touré, or David Silva.

City weathered the storm in the opening minutes, stayed compact, benefited from the absence of a center forward to finish off the excellent chances that Roma were creating, and little by little started turning things around until they had seized possession and position and made Nasri's superb goal count to take them through to the next round.

But Barça was waiting for them in the next round, and although three different managers had sat on the bench in the previous three seasons at the Camp Nou, the main ideas remained in place, and changing the Catalan team's roles isn't so easy.

City's defeat in that stage showed that, as they never came up against a team which dominated possession so much (in England such a team simply does not exist), they didn't know how to react when they weren't controlling the game. After Bayern the previous year, it was the second season in a row where they had been given a lesson under the noses of their own fans.

It also gave observers the feeling that Pellegrini didn't know how to click into Champions League mode. A two-legged tie isn't played the same tactically or mentally as the group games. You have to be patient, and, without losing your own identity, time needs to be seen differently. Even more so if you have a giant on the other side of the halfway line.

PELLEGRINI'S LAST SEASON—THE FINAL DECLINE

Manuel Pellegrini couldn't really say very much against being replaced by Guardiola. As time went by, Manchester City became a more splintered team, less solid in midfield and increasingly ineffective in finding solutions to the problems they came up against.

Pellegrini inherited a team from Mancini that had a well-founded philosophy, a squad full of top players, and financial backing which few clubs in the world could match, but the results didn't follow. If it hadn't been for Gerrard's slip they would never have won the Premier League, and the only year they got farther than the last sixteen in the Champions League they didn't produce very much and weren't able to overcome a faltering and insipid Real Madrid.

When he replaced Yaya Touré with a more defensive midfielder, like Fernando when they were down 3-0 against Leicester City, it was clear that Pellegrini had realized just how poor his side's midfield was.

And this didn't only happen in this game; it was a recurring pattern throughout the 2015-2016 season.

If City's midfield had been as strong as before they wouldn't have gone four months without a win away from home in the Premier League. They had the weapons to still be effective, but the arrival of Kevin De Bruyne and Raheem Sterling made them a more direct team and less inclined to keep possession.

To make matters worse, the continual injuries to Fabian Delph, who was perhaps the perfect player to recover the fluency and autonomy in the midfield, stopped him from being a part of the team, which contributed greatly to an even more pronounced and irreversible decline.

When you're facing a very well-organized team strong in defense and plays on the counter, your midfield solidity allows you to keep your opponents in their own half and minimize the risk of being caught on the counter. On that day, Leicester played a perfect defensive game, and Manchester City offered no real threat in attack, so not dominating the most important area of the pitch contributed to their not enjoying parity in the battle.

Yaya Touré showed that his form was in free fall, and the signs offered throughout the season were very clear. It was like the end of a symbiotic relationship between the team and its star midfielder; both stopped feeding, and they dragged each other toward the edge of a precipice.

A game which fairly clearly showed the profound changes Manchester City underwent in Manuel Pellegrini's last season was their visit to Liverpool on March 2, just three days after beating them on penalties in the League Cup final.

Yaya Touré and Kevin De Bruyne were injured and Pellegrini started with Fernando and Fernandinho in midfield, and Silva, Navas, Sterling, and Kun Agüero in attack. When they came in at half-time down 2-0 down a terrible first half by Sterling, Pellegrini decided to replace him with Wilfried Bony. However, with no visible reaction after ten minutes of the second half, he took Fernandinho off and put Kelechi Iheanacho on, ending up with three forwards.

While this could be seen as a clear attempt to go for the three points on offer, the reading of these substitutions also has a less obvious angle. Manchester City's midfield was more and more fragile, and now, with Fernando as its only member, Pellegrini had just weakened it even more.

The energy of Jordan Henderson and Emre Can and the support of James Milner had shorted the circuits between Fernando and Fernandinho, who, without Yaya, were left feeling even more naked.

The substitution was clearly an overreaction by Pellegrini. By having more forwards on the pitch you're not necessarily going to have more goal-scoring opportunities, and City's problem at that time wasn't missing chances, but the obvious surrender of the ball in midfield.

Just minutes after taking Fernandinho off, City lost the ball in the sensitive midfield area and was completely defenseless against Liverpool's attacking transition. Roberto Firmino knocked in the third goal. There was no way back and Pellegrini watched as his attempt to chase the game became the final nail in the coffin.

It wasn't a question of bad luck; it was the fair result for his substitutions and for how Manuel Pellegrini couldn't arrest the breakdown of his midfield, the side's most important treasure, which had kept them compact and provided their recovery after a small bad run.

Manchester City never had identity problems or long runs of bad results because there was something which wouldn't allow it. It's no coincidence that this was City's worst season in years, because their most solid point had fallen to its lowest ebb.

With substitutions like that, Pellegrini made it clear that he didn't know what the real problems in his team were and that he didn't have the resources to find a coherent response. Once again, he was a plan A manager; if this failed, everything fell apart.

Yaya Touré was less and less influential in midfield, and the presence of Raheem Sterling didn't fit in with the possession game which had been City's identifying feature in the previous few years. The system splintered, there was no longer the same pressure after the ball had been lost, and even when Fernando, Fernandinho, and Yaya Touré were playing, the team didn't have the same levels of quality possession or dominance. They were, quite simply, just another stone in the mountain.

The defeat at Southampton and the draw at Newcastle in the season run-in, together with many other tepid performances, showed that Manchester City didn't have a team ready to cope with the demands of the final stages of the season.

Taking care of a top-four place and heading safely to the Champions League was asking too much of them. It was like trying to cover yourself with a short blanket that leaves your head or your feet sticking out because it won't cover your whole body.

The defense is another one of the lines which came crashing down in the blink of an eye. Vincent Kompany spent almost the whole season injured, and the other center backs didn't perform at the level the competition required. Perhaps we can't blame Nicolás Otamendi too much because it was his first season in the squad, but Eliaquim Mangala didn't come close to living up to the expectations the club had for him or the price tag they paid for him.

Pellegrini didn't then go out of his way to help his defense by strengthening the midfield. Yaya Touré had lost his previous vitality, and although Manchester City used three midfielders in several games, this "overpopulation" didn't translate into defensive support.

Spaces were constantly created between the midfield and the defense, such as the one which allowed Marcus Rashford to score in the derby, or the one which Adam Lallana used to score the first of the three City conceded at Anfield, even with Kompany on the pitch.

A reliable second forward didn't emerge either. Bony had been a failure, Džeko went to Roma in the summer, and too much could not be asked of Iheanacho as he was only nineteen years old. The dependence on Kun Agüero had become greater than ever.

Jesús Navas didn't score a single goal in the Premier League in the last two seasons, Sterling didn't contribute much in that respect either, and while De Bruyne did so relatively frequently, when he got injured nobody else was able to step up and fill that void.

No wonder Manchester City's Premier League goal-scoring account decreased in Manuel Pellegrini's three seasons from 102 in the first season, when they were champions, to 83 in the second season, and 71 in the last.

There were too many problems which the Chilean was unable to control, just as he was unable to find a plan B that could offer an alternative to the team's primary formation. He didn't know how to maintain his players' motivation levels, and the landslide was hastened with the announcement of his departure.

In a team with so many physical and footballing problems, the one thing which mustn't be lost is motivation. Unfortunately, Pellegrini doesn't seem to be a great motivator—at least not in English.

THE ANNOUNCEMENT OF GUARDIOLA'S IMMINENT ARRIVAL—THE GREATEST NAIVETY

As if the structural problems Manchester City had were not enough, neither Manuel Pellegrini nor the wise (?) members of the board knew how to handle the announcement of Guardiola's arrival. The rumors in the press had destabilized the team's already turbulent situation, and Pellegrini thought that getting everything out in the open would help the storm to blow over. But it just made it bigger.

> *"I don't want to use [this] as an excuse but it was so difficult to work after that. Not for me, for the players," the Chilean said after the season had ended. And he added: "If I ask if I would do that again...I have some doubts."*[19]

Unfortunately, the media today invents all kinds of stories in order to sell copy, and in England the journalists have more contacts and more imagination than anywhere else. When it became known that Guardiola wasn't going to continue at Bayern, all eyes inevitably turned in unison to the bench at the Etihad, where the current incumbent was finding it indescribably difficult to lead the team along a safe road.

Which players will leave? Which ones will be marginalized? Which ones will need to improve or run the risk of not playing much? All these questions started to fall like sharp spears on the Manchester City squad while its players were negotiating the most difficult part of the season. From that moment, the players' minds began to stray more to the next season than the one which still had several months left to run.

Concentration disappeared in a puff of smoke, and City lost two games against Leicester and Tottenham Hotspur, two teams which happened to finish above them in the league.

A team which is inconsistent, which finds it very difficult to win away from home, which doesn't tread firmly in the race for the title, which has defensive problems and whose captain is repeatedly injured. A team which doesn't have a goal-scorer to back up Kun Agüero and which sees that Yaya Touré isn't exerting the same influence in midfield, or in attack, or in offering a balance, or in protecting a weak defense. Is that the right time to add another reason for players, and even for himself, to worry?

Pellegrini, when he found out that he wouldn't be continuing, was to lose the will to fight to the last breath. In the end, what was the point? Jupp Heynckes did something similar when he announced he'd be leaving Bayern Munich in 2013, but it was a completely different situation. That Bayern was a well-oiled machine mentally and in footballing terms, the news was received differently, and their manager, interestingly also replaced by Guardiola, was putting an end to his career as a personal decision, not one which had been forced upon him.

Sometimes football isn't as professional as it appears, and the senseless decisions made by clubs come back to haunt them. The Manchester City management, including Pellegrini, showed a great immaturity in not keeping the change in managers secret and not realizing that its announcement would only serve to demotivate everyone.

Were they expecting something different? What is Pellegrini going to think if he's told six months beforehand that he's going to be replaced at the end of the season? Would it not have been a little more professional to have kept it secret and announced it once everything had finished? Then we would have accused them of plotting the arrival of Guardiola behind Pellegrini's back, but it would have been a different sort of "crime"—a betrayal perhaps, similar to that of Manchester United with Mourinho and van Gaal—but at least it wouldn't have been such a display of naivety.

Pellegrini left Guardiola with a very complex situation, because the team had lost its essence to an alarming degree, and now Pep was going to need to employ more resources from his arsenal to drive through his game based on possession and maintaining positions on the pitch, without creating so much as a whiff of any tactical chaos. He would need an extra effort in terms of persuasion and mental strength to inculcate the style he's never going to abandon into his players. The work Guardiola would do would show us how deep Mancini's seed was sown and how resistant it has been to all the attacks it's been subjected to in the last few seasons.

Pep was going to need to rebuild a midfield—his favorite area of the pitch—which was once the most dominant in the Premier League almost from scratch. Until then, Manchester City had recovered quite convincingly in those periods when they'd lost their midfield strength, but this was a completely different chapter in the story.

Playing with a style based on possession again wasn't going to be too much of a problem for Manchester City, but Pep needed to rethink how to make that sensitive area of the pitch the most influential part of his team again.

From the moment he arrived, Guardiola made it clear that he wanted to base City's game on building solidly from the back and that he was planning to spread the midfield to areas of the pitch which didn't traditionally belong to it. He therefore made it clear that Fernandinho was able to play in several positions and to participate in the build-up play from an area as far back as central defense, because he was able to play precise passes forward.

> *"We need to create good build-up play, with easy passes in midfield, to achieve good passes for our strikers further up the pitch," said Guardiola in one of his first press conferences.*[20]

Manchester City won their first ten games of the season, and the magical touch of their new manager seemed to be in evidence. He'd revived the team overnight with a few chats, intense training sessions, and a few official games. Indeed, even with the loss of Ilkay Gündoğan, it was David Silva and Kevin De Bruyne who bolstered the less attack-minded part of the midfield, strengthening a brilliant attack–defense dual function and making people think that City were able to play almost perfectly, even without their full squad available.

But the first cracks began to appear in the second game of the group stage of the Champions League against Celtic in Glasgow and continued with the visit of Tottenham Hotspur, a team which has shown excellent progression and has acquired a well-defined style with Mauricio Pochettino. Spurs showed a lot of self-confidence, and this allowed Pochettino to get around the absence of Harry Kane, who was injured, without a definite number 9. Manchester City was never manifestly superior in any area of the pitch and succumbed due to defensive slips by Otamendi and Kolarov and the brilliant anticipation of the Tottenham players.

Then the magical world which seemed to be emerging at the Etihad Stadium, which was very much in keeping with the aura Guardiola himself had built in his previous clubs, started to look a little different.

One of the areas managers try to keep under control is the extent of the unpredictable. This sport brings with it a large amount of luck, the effects of which only the finest work and very few teams are able to minimize. Guardiola, until now, had demonstrated a peerless ability to fight against it, but he found himself in a situation which was completely new to him.

With the promised land of the first ten games now becoming a blur in the distance behind them, Manchester City embarked on a critical run of results. However, Guardiola didn't think there was a particular crisis, and he transmitted this message to his players after the draw at home against Southampton on October 23 when he locked himself in the dressing room with them for forty minutes. "*We cannot doubt,*" he told them, "*that the path we have chosen* [or I have chosen?] *is the right one, and that is not the problem.*"[21]

On December 3, Manchester City showed their wobbly side again when they lost at home to a Chelsea team who was very clinical when it came to taking advantage of their rival's defensive horrors. City left incredible spaces in their defense, spaces which Guardiola must have warned them about in the various prematch meetings, but that communication didn't seem to be evident on the pitch.

The most worrying thing was that the tactical and defensive mess started to have an emotional impact. It was the first time in his career that Guardiola had faced such a long period of instability. He hadn't confronted these problems at Barça or at Bayern and, naturally, he was finding it difficult to find a way through them.

One of the perennial wishes of Guardiola is that the players in his team should be able to play in more than one position. Midfielders, because they play in an area of the pitch which is in permanent contact with adjacent positions, have a greater tendency to acquire the skills which need to be inherent in order to be versatile. If a holding midfielder is good at passing the ball forward, can protect the ball, and knows how to press effectively high up the pitch, then it's very likely that Guardiola will consider him as a central defender, as was his intention with Fernandinho.

Another example of this was later in the season with Aleksandar Kolarov—although perhaps he meets few of these criteria—whom he used on a number of occasions for the poor performances of his starting partnership of John Stones and Nicolás Otamendi. He did the same with Fernandinho, using him as a full back on both flanks because of his hard work and devotion in following instructions.

The idea of putting Fernandinho on the flank had a hidden benefit, as he covered as a full back when the team didn't have the ball, and he had to move there to defend, but Guardiola's real intention was to give him the responsibility of bringing the ball out from the back when the team started the offensive transition—which the center backs weren't able to do to Guardiola's standards—and then he made him quietly move into the midfield to strengthen that area and enhance a more effective recovery of the ball farther away from City's own goal.

However, it turned out that City didn't dominate possession as much and wasn't as skillful when it came to controlling opponents' counterattacks, and this meant that Fernandinho's dual role of full back–midfielder was reduced to just the former, and he was forced to cover the flank quickly to avoid the opponent taking possession of those spaces.

Similar options didn't produce a dramatic change in City's play, instead just being a palliative solution and papering over the cracks.

Manchester City lost two games in a row in December: 1-3 at home to Chelsea and 4-2 away to Leicester City. John Stones couldn't stop making mistakes, but Kolarov couldn't get it right either when he replaced him at center back in a back four, or as left center back in a back three. Against Arsenal on December 18, Guardiola left Stones on the bench and started Kolarov at center back. After five minutes, Theo Walcott raced through that side like an arrow and scored with ease. How was John Stones then supposed to gain confidence and develop the game Guardiola wanted? Kolarov isn't going to be playing as an improvised center back next season. Everything seemed to point to Guardiola wanting to end the season with as little damage as possible in order to start rebuilding from scratch in the summer with new players in those positions.

It is often heard, even in the media, that a manager needs X number of transfer windows in order to have the team he wants. But what should a manager do—sign players to suit his style and tactical demands, or adapt to what he has and try to build a competitive team? It depends on the team and the finances available, of course, but the great majority of managers can't sign all the players they would like because their clubs don't have the resources to do so. Everyone would love to have a Buffon in goal, a Maldini in defense, a Vieira in midfield, and three Messis up front. But that's a privilege few can afford. Generally, then, it's more likely that teams will have to create their own type of football rather than being able to buy it ready-made. When Guardiola arrived at Manchester City, perhaps he tried to strike a balance between the two without spending disproportionately, but the experiment failed.

For example, we might say that Antonio Conte is tactically a little one-dimensional, because when Chelsea lost two games in a row with a back four he quickly changed the team formation and started playing with three center backs. Conte came up against a problem, and he solved it with the players he had in the squad at the time; he didn't need to buy anyone to lead Chelsea to the Premier League title. Conte tried things out, made adjustments, saw what worked, and ended up winning the championship without making any hugely drastic innovations, like those Guardiola tried at Manchester City.

In the summer, Guardiola didn't want to replace several footballers who were coming into the final year on their contracts. He preferred to see what Bacary Sagna, Pablo Zabaleta, and Gaël Clichy could offer. He didn't want to move the squad around too much or buy a new team, but the club left him in a difficult situation when it allowed so many players to reach the final year of their contracts without there being a clear intention to renew them. The mentality of those players when they found out that they would be leaving the next year wasn't in keeping with the commitment Pep demands or with the long-term vision a project as ambitious as his entails.

Perhaps now Pep regrets not having been more dynamic and not having brought in a couple of suitable men for the task, but the preseason and the initial ten victories deceived him, blinded him, made him see an oasis which changed overnight into a well of moving sands. Sir Alex Ferguson put it into words in his excellent book, *Leading*: "*Jimmy Sirrell ... taught me a crucial lesson. He told me never to let all the players' contracts expire around the same time*."[22]

It suddenly seemed like Guardiola had lost the ability to get his players to understand his philosophy and carry it out. It wasn't just a question of the tough opponents he was coming up against in the most difficult league he'd managed in during his short career, but of what his own team was capable of doing for itself. The opponent is important, but it felt like even if this Manchester City had played in Spain or the Bundesliga, he would still have been at sea.

Pep's idea is indeed to play a style of football with the same principles that marked his time at Barça and Bayern, although not necessarily the same style. In the book *Herr Pep*, an account of his first year at Bayern, Guardiola says: "*I have to adapt to them. ... The most important thing are the players and the tactics must be adapted to them. In the final year at Barça, for example, we changed the whole system so that Cesc Fàbregas could come in.*"[23]

But now at Manchester City, when he put only one tough midfielder on defensive duties—instead of doing so with Yaya Touré and Fernandinho—and used David Silva and Kevin De Bruyne in a mixed role with defensive as well as attacking responsibilities, even though they had never played in that way before, is that really adapting to the footballers he has? Or is Guardiola so intransigent that he won't countenance playing with a very functional 4–2–3–1, which City played with for almost all of Manuel Pellegrini's three years? Introducing a 4–3–3 at that point and in that situation was like using a sledgehammer to crack a nut.

In the first games of the season, when Guardiola marginalized Yaya Touré, he only had Fernandinho as a holding midfielder, and he played Kevin De Bruyne almost next to him. Maybe De Bruyne regarded this role as an interim one, which he would have to take on to solve a temporary situation, and considered that if he did it well it would then enhance his standing as a player. In the first games of the season, Manchester City therefore played a very effective and attractive form of football, and De Bruyne felt highly motivated and completed his defensive duties excellently, without forgetting to go forward. He had a lot of energy, he wanted to impress Guardiola, and he was willing to do whatever he was asked.

However, Yaya Touré's marginalization continued, Gündoğan was injury prone, and De Bruyne started to realize that playing so deep and with such little influence going forward was becoming his main role. Little by little his forays forward were getting less frequent, and he was restricted to midfield duties, but perhaps without the complete desire to do this. David Silva, who has a higher standing in the team because of the length of time he's been at Manchester City and because of his own need to have the ball at his feet in order to feel alive on the pitch, wasn't so unhappy about having to participate so much in winning the ball back because doing so meant he was then getting more time with the ball.

De Bruyne, on the other hand, is a player who depends more on speed, on running into space, on not feeling so enclosed by playing at the base of the midfield. That's why David Silva "survived" the new duties Guardiola bestowed upon them better than De Bruyne, with the coach's refusal to play with two natural holding midfielders, which was perhaps the most feasible option to ensure the team's stability.

When Pep put Fernandinho and Fabian Delph in midfield against Chelsea on April 5, Silva played farther forward as the true *playmaker* that he is, and he caused so many problems that Antonio Conte brought on Nemanja Matić in the second half just to control Silva's influence. City lost, but Silva played to the best of his considerable ability.

After the various setbacks in the first months of the season, Guardiola hesitated to impose the style he wanted, and the phase where he rediscovered what was best for the team took longer than expected. Against Barça in the group stage of the Champions League, he left Kun Agüero out of the starting eleven because he said he wanted more midfielders, supposedly because he didn't want to give Barça an advantage in that area of the pitch, and he paid a heavy price: They lost 4-0. Manchester City failed to keep the ball when they were under intense pressure. The team wasn't fully organized to support each other and not give the ball away in situations they wouldn't usually, which hadn't happened in Guardiola's other teams.

For Pep, the Claudio Bravo fiasco was a major surprise which wasn't only down to the Chilean keeper's own performances, but also to the poor contributions of the defense as a whole. The center backs and full backs were also unable to transfer the ball well from the back and so the midfielders were forced to create a midfield for themselves, without much support from the players in the surrounding areas.

A midfield is basically made up of midfielders, but on their own they're nothing; they need the help of the closest players, and this was perfectly demonstrated in the game against Liverpool on December 31. City naively gave easy balls away and showed how weak they have become at dominating matches through a solid control of the midfield.

When a team's defensive line is positioned on the halfway line, as was the case with Guardiola's Barça and Bayern, the team is more compact, and the "midfield" is reduced to a few meters. Pep tried getting the City center backs to position themselves there, but the space they left behind them was easy pickings for their opponents, who waited in ambush for the moment to attack those open fields. This hit him hard, because there's nothing Guardiola hates more than being counterattacked. However, were those center backs adequately prepared to play like that?

If we also add that during the most crucial period of the season Bravo didn't save a shot at goal, then getting in behind the defense meant having a free run on goal. On December 10 against a Leicester City team struggling for a win, the Manchester City defense conceded three goals in twenty minutes. That day, Vardy was again the horse that Ranieri had described the previous season, galloping across the fields on offer in the City defense and scored a hat trick.

Manchester City had no identity, there was no balance between the lines, and Guardiola's methodical training, which had squeezed the best performances out of his players at Barça and Bayern, wasn't in evidence on the pitch. However much he said that he knew he was coming to a more difficult and special league, even he couldn't see how difficult he would find it not only to get good results, but also for the team to bear his stamp (or any stamp), an intention, and a balance between its defensive play and its attack. A team that would look like a Guardiola team.

This poor collective performance had a tactical and a mental component. The players and the manager didn't speak the same language, and Guardiola didn't want to use another language; he only has one, and he'll keep going with it until the players decipher his codes and are able to speak it. For the first time, a team of his wasn't able to efficiently reduce the role that luck plays in football. Insecurity also played its part and robbed several players of their courage and confidence.

It was getting difficult for Guardiola to find solutions to the lack of a connection between his players. The repeated absences of Kun Agüero through suspension and Gündoğan through injury had stopped him from establishing continuity in his lineups. Yaya Touré's level of performance wasn't the same as before, and in the most sensitive area of the midfield the outlook was far from encouraging. De Bruyne, because he had to play so deep and didn't bear so much attacking responsibility, started to lose the ability to find the lines to pass through and the channels to run into and score. His number of assists plummeted. Silva suffocated from having so much defensive responsibility and from his teammates' drop in performance levels.

A defeat is much more difficult to digest when it happens rarely. Manchester City shone in the first ten games of the season with their results and their level of play—as well as in finding alternatives to cover for the suspended Agüero, as in the spectacular victory over Manchester United on September 10—but after that, six games followed without a win precisely because the instability a game without a win creates is greater when this doesn't usually happen.

Because of this, from the psychological point of view, for a manager it's always important to make players believe that they aren't invincible, so that they don't live in a bubble which, if it bursts, will end up bursting them as well. Even if they win game after game, they should always remain aware that that rhythm won't last forever and that experiencing a defeat is normal, inevitable, and sometimes even necessary. Guardiola is eternally dissatisfied, a perfectionist even when it comes to constructing perfection, and he shouldn't have made a mistake when it came to motivating the Manchester City squad and working to improve even things which couldn't be improved, but in a way he ended up paying the price inherent in winning so many games. Paradoxically.

There's no single way to raise the performance levels of a team that has gotten stuck. While putting three men in midfield and looking for defensive solidity may be the most advisable and the most commonly used solution, there are no rules to point the way. Guardiola remained faithful to his idea of attack, attack, attack, whatever the cost, and he opted for a lot of attacking players and fewer defensive players, despite the fact that his defense wasn't watertight. Could it be that he didn't want to stray too far from the English footballing culture in order not to be such an outsider, as he had been in Germany? Perhaps the Bundesliga could be won by attacking, attacking, attacking because almost all teams there play like that, but England is a different story.

Guardiola asked his forwards at City for more sacrifice in order to compensate for the lack of more natural midfielders. In the game on February 5 against inferior opposition such as Swansea, those forwards weren't going to have to drop back to the edge of their own penalty area too much to get the ball, because most of the time the immediate press after losing it would be successful in winning it back, or else Swansea wouldn't be skillful enough to reach the Manchester City area very often.

However, against opponents who manage the ball better, who force them back and cause greater disorganization and physical exertion, would that formation offer City the coherence Guardiola dreamed of and the team needed to achieve positive results? Against Liverpool on March 19 and against Arsenal on April 2, Guardiola played with just one natural holding midfielder, and they drew both games. Even against Swansea, despite winning 2-1, it was a real struggle. Guardiola tried to turn the Manchester City ship around by going back to what he'd done in the first games of the season—when they'd gone on that unbeaten run—and returning to the super-attacking lineup with De Bruyne very close to the defensive midfielder and David Silva trying to be a playmaker when the team had the ball and a mixed midfielder when they lost it. But you're never as motivated after you've received a few setbacks, and although he used the same system again, now things didn't go as they had before.

The arrival of Gabriel Jesus in January showed just how dissatisfied Guardiola was with Kun Agüero. The fact that he started with a nineteen-year-old boy who'd just arrived from halfway across the world, who was not yet familiar with his work philosophy and with whom he'd only spent a few hours, shows how desperate he was to find a solution to the team's failings. Pep never got tired of repeating that the poor defense was a result of a poor attack and of not being able to take advantage of the many opportunities they were creating in front of goal. Agüero guarantees goals, but Guardiola demands goals and a level of commitment that the Argentine forward was apparently unable to offer. Agüero became another one of the list of players that Pep didn't try to mold to his principles or adapt to what he considers to be the best for the team (Eto'o, Ibrahimović, Mandžukić). He simply opted for marginalizing him, until life, capricious to the end, decided to injure Gabriel Jesus, and he had no choice but to put Agüero back in the starting eleven.

Gabriel Jesus could easily never have exploded onto the scene, and then Guardiola might have ended up regretting things if he couldn't come around to Agüero's "lack of dirty work." He hadn't asked it of Messi at Barça. Agüero is perhaps the Messi of Manchester City.

Another example occurred in the Champions League. Knowing that Monaco was the highest-scoring team in the five big European leagues, with an average of approximately three goals per game, Pep decided to stick to the formula of all-out attack and to come out playing from the back, even when it might have terrible consequences given his defense's inability to do so.

On several occasions, Manchester City gave away easy balls in their own half of the pitch, including once when Willy Caballero gifted Monaco a goal in the first leg. But Guardiola continued to give them the order to do so. Monaco's collapse in the final minutes of the game allowed Manchester City to win 5-3.

In the return leg, aware that Monaco had already scored three away goals, Guardiola didn't modify his super-attacking approach, even though perhaps the more advisable approach would be to try and manage the two-goal advantage they'd gained after the first ninety minutes. If you go toe-to-toe with Monaco you can get caught off-guard. This wasn't the right time to feed his ego; instead, he needed to turn to the safest formula.

Manchester City played one of their worst first halves of the season in Monaco. They created no danger, they didn't have a shot on goal, and their forwards didn't link up in the final third of the pitch as Guardiola likes, largely because they were so focused on defending that when they attacked they did so entirely chaotically. Maybe fatigue from the accumulation of games and the exertion that was expected of them in each game affected those attacking players.

It was no fluke that Monaco was leading the French league; they were a very well-drilled, well-tuned, precise, and very confident side. It's very difficult to beat a team like that with an approach which has not yet produced good, sustained results and which doesn't offer the required minimum level of security.

On that day, Guardiola preferred not to use his true midfielders. He left Yaya Touré and Fabian Delph on the bench and played Fernandinho as a natural midfielder, and, as Gaël Clichy admitted after the game, in the first half the players who were on the pitch were never able to put Guardiola's tactical instructions into practice. Pep had a master plan in mind, but he hadn't factored in the limited likelihood of those players being able to execute it on the pitch.

Guardiola is a person who finds the way his team plays more important than their winning. Of course, he wants both, but deep down he prefers the *how* over the *what* and sometimes that conspires against him. That's what he said in the press conference minutes after being knocked out by Monaco: "*It doesn't matter if we win or lose, but we have to be what we are – respect our style, our strengths*."[24]

Some days later, in the press conference before the Liverpool game, Pep said that he felt entirely responsible for the defeat against Monaco because he tried to convince his players to play in a particular way, but he couldn't because he's still getting to know the squad. So, if he's getting to know them and he knows that they haven't completely taken on his philosophy, why does he force them to play like that in such an important game with so little margin for error? Why not plump for a safer approach, which would make the players feel better on the pitch and which would allow them to make the most of the two-goal advantage from the first leg?

In the book *Herr Pep*, after the overwhelming 0-4 home defeat Bayern Munich suffered at the hands of Real Madrid in the Champions League semi-final in 2014, Guardiola made a similar revelation: "*The only way I know to win is to play well, as I understand playing well, which is to fill the midfield and to pass the ball much more to each other*."[25] His regrets came from having chosen an anti-Guardiola lineup for such an important game, with a lot of forwards and not many midfielders, despite the fact that during the whole season he'd encouraged a style based on controlling the midfield. At that time, according to him, he preferred to go for the game and was led more by his heart than his head, more by abandon than tactical order, and life dealt him his biggest failure until then. It's incredible that Guardiola didn't remember that episode and make the right decision against Monaco, even when he was two goals up from the first leg.

For example, if we go back to the brilliant victory on September 10 against Manchester United at Old Trafford with Kun Agüero missing through suspension, Guardiola did play with two defensive midfielders in the closing stages of the game, and he managed to maintain the score line.

That day he started with Kelechi Iheanacho as center forward, Fernandinho as the only holding midfielder, and four attacking midfielders. But when City was ahead 2-1 and United was throwing everything at them in search of the equalizer, the substitution of Iheanacho with Fernando, although on paper a seemingly ultra-defensive one, aimed to reorganize the team, make it more solid in midfield and simply vary the means of attack.

Iheanacho doesn't have the finishing potency of Agüero to be a real threat in front of goal; nor does he have the ability to drop back to the halfway line, help out in defense, and join in the team's counterattacks, which was how Pep was being forced to play at that point. Because of this, and on seeing that Manchester United was intensifying its pressure, that substitution seemed very logical and one he had to make.

Guardiola changed to play with a midfield with two more defensive elements and four attackers, although none of these was a center forward. However, those attackers—Silva, De Bruyne, Nolito, and Sterling (and his replacement, Sané)—had enough skill to form an attacking alliance without causing their firepower to dwindle too much. It was a risky change, of course, but as Pep said after the game, they couldn't control everything. He took the risk, Fernando had a tremendous second half, and City took all three points.

A little pragmatic, a little risky, but City kept its firepower, calmed the United storm and also created several goal-scoring opportunities to finish the game off on the counter. It wasn't an easy game, and they were never going to score a hat-full of goals; instead, it was a game that would be decided by fine margins. Guardiola was very astute and got his reward.

The change of Fernando for Iheanacho turned out to be a very valid resource given the situation of the game, and it was also laudable that he didn't start the game without a natural number 9. The option of a false 9 was never his plan A, and even though he didn't have his first-choice number 9, he decided to trust the reserve.

But against Monaco, it was a completely different story. Pep had mutated to a phase where he wanted to force his style on his players instead of introducing it passively and with intelligence. He wasn't adapting to them, and instead he wanted to force them to adapt to him.

As had happened at Bayern Munich, Guardiola's style of football clashed when he brought it to England. The way he plays is not one that is common in the Premier League, although Manchester City in recent years had played football based on the principles of dominating possession as a fundamental weapon.

However, Leroy Sané and Raheem Sterling are not Arjen Robben and Franck Ribéry; they don't have the tactical mastery or the finishing ability to embody the same roles. Using Kevin De Bruyne as a midfielder had the same effect as when Guardiola tried to do the same thing with Thomas Müller at Bayern. Disastrous.

Chapter 5

THE TRANSFORMATIONS IN BARÇA AFTER THE ARRIVAL OF GUARDIOLA

In order to have a better understanding of the possibility of Manchester City flourishing again under Guardiola, we should look no further than his work at Barça, a team which fed from the same seed of ball possession, but which Frank Rijkaard had impoverished in the two preceding seasons.

Guardiola took charge in 2008, fired motivation levels through the roof, exploited the individual strengths of every player, put these at the disposal of the team, and built one of the greatest legends in the history of football. And all from his very first season.

That magical Barça side reduced the role luck had to play to an absolute minimum because they controlled each facet of the game in an endless cycle of attack and defense. These were times of footballing perfection, but Guardiola knew that eventually their opponents would find the antidote, so he couldn't assume that the same formation and the same style of play would remain unbeatable forever. So, what did he do in order to redesign the Catalan side?

In his second season Pep experienced the huge failure of signing Zlatan Ibrahimović, a player he had requested himself as a replacement for one he had never wanted, Samuel Eto'o, even though the Cameroonian scored thirty-six goals in the treble season, which was the only one they spent together.

Guardiola hadn't realized that Ibrahimović wasn't a player who could move to the wing like Eto'o or David Villa, and that he wouldn't be willing to abandon his position as center forward. It's clear that there wasn't too much communication between Pep and Ibra before his signing, and the possible pros and cons of his arrival at the Camp Nou hadn't been explored. It was a blind signing, and the result, as expected, wasn't healthy at all.

Guardiola wasn't prepared to take Messi's role of central reference point in attack away from him, and Messi wasn't ready to give it up. A few seasons later it became clear that this wasn't an unreasonable idea, as a more peripheral Messi was able to live together with Neymar and Luis Suárez in the Barça side which also won the treble in 2015 and the League and Copa del Rey in 2016.

On one occasion, a Spanish journalist suggested that Guardiola masterfully drew up a plan to build a suitable habitat where Messi could exploit his great strengths as the center of the Barcelona universe. It's true that Messi's goal-scoring record was great and needed to be protected, but all the other players in the team also had to play second fiddle to him. A team is never based around one player; quite the reverse, if the player is so great and versatile, it's he who should put his skills at the disposal of the team.

Messi performed well when he started off on the wing, as he has also done as a playmaker, and he exploded as a center forward. So why not use his versatility to help other players perform who aren't so multifunctional but are able to do very well in areas which converge with Messi's habitat at that time? Football is a team sport, and individuals, no matter how great they are, should always play for the good of the team.

Although sometimes getting the best out of one player might make a whole team perform to its very best ability, this isn't always the case. Guardiola protected Messi's environment too much and encouraged the other forwards to respect his privileged, untouchable position. That's why Ibrahimović didn't work, and why Villa only half-worked; that's why Alexis Sánchez didn't explode as he did at Udinese and Arsenal, and it wasn't until Messi moved a little farther back on the pitch—as he did after the arrival of Neymar and Luis Suárez—that the team started playing at full throttle again. Even then, in the treble year of 2015, Messi scored more league goals than Suárez and Neymar combined (thirty-eight), although this was the Uruguayan's first season, when he was adapting; the following year he was the league's top scorer with forty goals.

Guardiola was still learning his trade as a manager in some matters, and this type of failure has never been repeated since in his career. Now he's much more meticulous when it comes to selecting his players, and, as he knows what he wants, his selection procedure is more efficient.

How did Pep resolve this skirmish on the pitch?

In that, his second season, he wasn't as consistent in his systems as he was in his first. At first, he no longer always used the 4–3–3 which had given him the footballing paradise of the previous season, and at times he played four central midfielders. For example, in the league game against Valencia at the Mestalla, he started with Yaya Touré, Seydou Keita, Xavi, and Iniesta, with Pedro and Messi up front.

In the second half, Barça laid siege to Valencia, completely dominated the match, and if Guardiola had put on another forward a win would have followed, as they just needed a little more finishing prowess in the area, but he didn't, and the game ended goalless.

Against Osasuna and Rubin Kazan he did the same thing and again didn't get the win.

The continual injuries to Ibrahimović, his increasing lack of goals, and Thierry Henry's poor form made it more difficult for him to find a balanced starting lineup, but this in no way justifies arriving at the Santiago Bernabéu, in the game which could have been a title decider, with Dani Alves as a winger and with Pedro and Messi alone up front, while Bojan Krkić was left on the bench after having such a great game against Athletic Bilbao just a few days before.

The tactical outcome was so bad that, in the second half, Guardiola shifted his defense around and moved Alves back to his natural position. But there were nearly sixty-five minutes in which a Barça *lite* wandered around the Santiago Bernabéu, and they could only extend their dominance over their great rival, because they were quite frankly helped by an inoffensive, faint-hearted, and off-key Real Madrid team, who ended up gifting them a 0-2 win.

However, one week later, Guardiola repeated the same formation in a difficult and away key game against Espanyol at Cornellá. Messi, Pedro, and Maxwell, now playing as a winger, were the three most advanced players. Barça created no threat at all, and after almost an hour, Pep went for a more natural 4–3–3 when he brought on Henry.

Ten minutes from the end, he decided to gamble on Ibrahimović, but after a very inconsistent season where he sometimes hadn't been able to make his presence felt on the pitch during entire matches, it was practically impossible for him to do so in such a short time.

Now, is a player really suitable to be picked if the team ends up needing him and he only gets to play for ten minutes? The final 0-0 score line was a fair result for the team Guardiola picked and for what it achieved on the pitch. A different Barça that had nothing in common with the machine of months before.

Three days later and, in a Europe clogged up by the ashes of the unpronounceable volcano in Iceland, the first leg of the Champions League semi-final against Inter Milan arrived together with perhaps the moment of the greatest tactical impudence in Guardiola's career. Losing 1-3, he took Ibrahimović off and put Eric Abidal on, moving Maxwell forward to his new position as a winger. Incredible, but true. Losing by two goals, he changed a forward for a defender in order to end the game with Piqué playing as center forward.

It was in that last half-hour of the first leg that Barça needed to reduce Inter's advantage in the tie. It was completely counterproductive to try and defend that "result" with the hope of turning the tie around at the Camp Nou.

Guardiola wanted Messi to start running with the ball thirty meters from goal and take it past three or four lines of world-class defenders like he did in the Spanish league against second-rate teams, instead of putting him closer to the box so that he could try to link with the players around him, or as a last resort try and draw a foul just outside the area, get a free kick, and force a red card for one of the opposition.

When your opponent surprises you and has you at a disadvantage, you need to be very clever and find the most unexpected ways, ways which are never used, to get a win. But Guardiola confused this with excessive innovation, and the moment he most needed to have his best players on the pitch in their proper positions was precisely when he didn't do so.

For the return leg, he left the two left backs, Abidal and Maxwell, on the bench, and played none other than Gabriel Milito in that position and Yaya Touré as a false center back. It would be interesting to see how much this formation had been practiced and how Milito had got on in the training games ahead of this match, because on the only two occasions he touched the ball in attack, it ended up going over the dead-ball line once and hitting the referee the other time.

No matter how much you try to understand this extremely innovative but senseless lineup, there isn't a grain of logic in it to suggest that it would ensure turning around a game that wasn't dissimilar to the last half-hour of the first leg. Barça was going to have the ball the vast majority of the time, and Inter was going to have no choice other than to sit back.

But Guardiola's starting lineup halted the magic of what could have been one of the epic nights of Barcelona's history, like the Gothenburg game in 1986, in its tracks.[26] The support campaign in the city, the "We will leave everything on the pitch" message after the Xerez game days before, and Piqué's announcement that the Inter players were going to hate their job while they were on the Camp Nou pitch all served for naught.

It's true that it's very difficult to find a way through a team that is tight at the back—as Barça and Guardiola had learned the year before at Stamford Bridge—but a second look at the match shows that there were spaces, but that Barça was never able to exploit them. The passes into the area were never good enough, and most of the time the ball was passed ineffectively and horizontally from the middle to the wings and back again, or was crossed for two superb center backs—Lúcio and Walter Samuel—to deal with. Just when Barça needed to be Barça, they were unable to be.

Messi never managed to dribble past his three compatriots, Zanetti, Walter Samuel, and Esteban Cambiasso, perhaps because they knew him, or perhaps because he needed some kind of distraction and protection that he never got. He didn't link with Ibrahimović; they didn't draw markers away from each other; and he showed a great lack of the sort of leadership games like this cry out for and which on the vast majority of occasions, although not always, he has shown.

After Thiago Motta's red card, when Inter had no choice but to pull back and try to weather the storm, Messi moved farther away from the goal. What he did most was to pass the ball, usually to Xavi, but not look for the return ball, which was one of the main goal-scoring weapons he'd employed since both players had started playing together in Barça's first team, just as they had a few days before in the game against Real Madrid.

The tie was lost in the first hour of the match in Milan, where Inter and Barcelona played an open game and scored four goals between them. But when the Italian team sat back for the rest of the game and for almost all of the second leg, in double the time only one goal was scored. When they played football, Inter was the better team, and Barça's ineffectiveness reached a climax with Ibrahimović's poor form and the great contrast with that of Samuel Eto'o the previous year and David Villa the following year.

The Emirates game against Arsenal in the quarter-finals, with fifteen minutes never seen before in the history of football between two great teams, was of little use. There are no records of a team having played like that away from home against another big European team, with such insolence and battering the opposition goal in the way that Barça did to Arsenal. It was something unique, unanswerable, which only they could repeat.

It was best described by Theo Walcott, who said: "*It was like someone was holding a PlayStation controller and moving the figures around.*"27

However, no team is unbeatable and no system unbreakable. The imperious need for evolution, the right evolution, was evident once more.

When a manager uses such a strange formation or such a crazy idea, he ends up overly exposing himself. If it turns out well, he may be considered a genius, but if not, he may be subjected to a lot of deserved criticism. Football is very unpredictable, and a manager must be aware of that. He must therefore protect himself by avoiding ideas which are too crazy and which will have an enormous effect on his reputation if they don't work. Indeed, if he does get the desired result it may not be entirely down to his "brilliance" but could be due to how luck falls in particular events that might happen in a given match.

The departure of Ibrahimović was inevitable, for the good of everyone: the team, the player himself, and Guardiola. However, although his replacement, David Villa, is Spanish and had been playing with many of the Barça squad in the national team for several years, the team was being exposed to first season syndrome again.

It's generally highly preferable to opt for a second season for the newcomer. Even the best players can have a bad first year, particularly if they join a club where they aren't the biggest name and where they have to adapt to an environment and an approach that are completely new for them.

In order to make the most of the weapons at their disposal, players, particularly forwards, may need time to bed in which could last anything from one day to two years. After two whole seasons, if the manager doesn't get what he was hoping for, he may think about making a change. In this case, Guardiola's own mistake in bringing in Zlatan forced him to look for a solution with a new signing.

After Messi's great goal-scoring season—thirty-four in the league and forty-seven in total, his first with really stratospheric numbers—Pep preferred to put Villa toward the left side a little and to keep the Argentinian as the player with the main responsibility for putting the ball in the back of the net.

Barça still didn't sign a forward in the Henrik Larsson mold, a player who arrived aged thirty-three, in good physical shape, and knowing beforehand what his role in the squad would be. He wasn't going to compete with the first-team regulars, but look for the minutes available through injuries or games where Barça was unable to find a way through.

This isn't a role that just any player could fill; it requires someone who wouldn't be hit psychologically and whose potency wouldn't be affected by so much time on the bench. It would particularly need to be a forward who offered something different to Guardiola's plan A, preferably a forward, like the Swede, who was strong in the air.

Nobody at the club saw the advantages of bringing in another player with these characteristics, which may partly have taken playing time away from Bojan, but which was necessary in the long run in order to break down the fortresses erected, for example, by Mourinho in the Champions League semi-final with Inter in 2010 and the Copa del Rey final with Real Madrid in 2011.

At times, Messi forgot about his goal-scoring role and retreated too far, leaving a lot of defensive lines to get past. He can dribble past one, two, but it's difficult for him to get past them all.

So why not leave the creative roles to the right people—Xavi and Iniesta—more so now that the team needed precise passes, and leave Messi farther forward to receive the ball as close to the opposition's area as possible?

With Villa's lack of goals, the team's goal-scoring burden fell entirely on the shoulders of Messi. The farther away he was from the goal, the less likely he was to score.

In the last three games where the opponents had put the barriers up at the back against Barça—Chelsea in the Champions League semi-final in 2009, Inter at the same stage the following year, and Real Madrid in the Copa del Rey final in 2011—Messi moved too far back, wanting to take over the direction of the game, when in reality he was needed closer to the front. In all those games Barça found it very difficult to score and was only able to do so in extremis in two of them. Xavi and Iniesta's ability to distribute the ball was minimal, as they fell victim to the opponents playing with two lines with very little space between them and with the members of those lines very close to each other.

It had become clear that this was the formula for beating Barça. It was now just a question of waiting for Guardiola and his coaching staff to find the antidote.

GUARDIOLA'S LAST SEASON—THE WRONG WAY

Pep realized that something needed to change, but his choice of what wasn't a happy one. In his last season he immersed himself more in the task of strengthening the team's central play with many midfielders with similar characteristics and few forwards. Guardiola showed his most stubborn side, Barça drew too many games and ended up handing the league to Real Madrid in 2012.

Fàbregas arrived, and that only served to slow down the wonderful progress Thiago Alcántara had made the previous season, when he emerged as the natural replacement for Xavi. That summer in the preseason Bayern tournament, Thiago had given a footballing recital and shown that he was ready to take on an increasingly leading role, but the signing of Fàbregas stopped the natural course of his development to the point that he ended up leaving the Camp Nou. The biggest contradiction in all this is that it was Guardiola himself who ended up rescuing him at Bayern.

Let's begin the review with the second league game of the season against Real Sociedad at the Anoeta, where Guardiola used Keita, Thiago Alcántara, Xavi, and Fàbregas in midfield, while Alexis and Pedro were the only forwards. Iniesta, Messi, and Villa were left on the bench, possibly being kept back for the first game in the group stage of the Champions League against AC Milan.

This league game was much more important, and the points on offer had more significance than a possible failure to win against the Italian side. Barça drew 2-2, and when he was asked about those three players being left out, Guardiola said, "*It's a good lesson for the future. I make the decisions, and I thought it was best.*"[28]

But it seems that the lesson wasn't really learned because, two games later, in another very difficult away game at Valencia—a game where only going with your best weapons will do—he again only played two forwards, Pedro and Messi, and he overpopulated the midfield with Keita, Busquets, Xavi, and Fàbregas. This showed that Guardiola wasn't going to give up so easily and would go to great lengths to prove that his idea could work.

Barça drew 2-2 again, and what's more, when they were losing 2-1 Guardiola only replaced Pedro with Villa. In other words, he didn't opt for going back to the 4–3–3 which had worked so well for him in the three previous seasons. He continued to use Cesc as a kind of free central midfielder who tried to make "surprise" runs from deep both in slow build-ups and swift counterattacks, but his contribution didn't make up for the absence of another natural forward.

Pep and the team had the misfortune of this being one of Messi's worst games in his career. The Argentinian assisted for both goals and played a tremendous pass for Villa which put him through on the keeper, but he made countless mistakes with simple passes and in the end did more wrong than right.

Barça's play was completely static, lacking speed, predictable, and they only really woke up in the last fifteen minutes when Valencia sat back in their own area.

It was already public knowledge that when Barça was faced with a team that sits back with two banks of four on the edge of the area, they get stuck. In this game, Valencia was winning and could afford the luxury of shutting up shop. Then the Catalan team had no choice other than to look for through balls. Messi played three—both goals and the one Villa missed—but he couldn't weave his way through because he wasn't given the chance to dribble, run, or shoot.

But this whole debacle was due largely to Barça only having two natural forwards up front. Messi played as a "10" and Pedro on the wing, but there was nobody in the center of the attack, so there was no goal threat. Fàbregas didn't come close to doing what had made him into that feared box-to-box central midfielder at Arsenal. He couldn't because he had too many players next to him, and he wasn't as influential at the Camp Nou as he had been at the Emirates Stadium. Now he was a little farther down the pecking order, and it's far from easy to shine when you're playing next to Messi, Iniesta, Xavi, and co.

In that game Barça didn't need another Xavi; they needed a number 9, or at least another winger to stretch the pitch and allow Messi to play very close to the area. David Villa was on the bench, but Guardiola made the conscious decision not to use him. With the lack of a third forward, Dani Alves was supposed to get up the right wing and attack more, but he did so very little. Valencia didn't give any opportunities away; they sat back and bit on the counterattack.

Normally, the harder the opponent you're facing, especially if you're playing away, the more you need to turn to your most powerful weapons. Guardiola had already seen clear evidence that on these difficult pitches the idea of playing with four midfielders and just two forwards wasn't working for him, but he still clung to it anyway.

The strange thing is that in apparently easy games at home Guardiola did play with three forwards, even though this meant including a kid from the B team in Isaac Cuenca. It was at home where he could allow himself a certain license, because the very fact of playing in front of their own fans meant Barcelona was playing with an extra man, but Pep clearly saw things differently.

In the twelfth game of the league season, Barcelona had to travel to another difficult ground, San Mamés, the home of Athletic Bilbao, who was managed by the brash and magical Marcelo Bielsa. Although Barça drew again—funnily enough it was again 2-2—and Guardiola started with Busquets, Xavi, Iniesta, Fàbregas, Adriano, and Messi, he was short of available forwards that day because Pedro was injured, while David Villa and Alexis Sánchez started on the bench, but they were on their way back from injuries and only played for a few minutes in the second half.

The battle for the league was well and truly joined, and Mourinho's Real Madrid was in the lead. Barça had to travel to the Santiago Bernabéu, and, predictably, Guardiola stuck to his four midfielders and two forwards, Alexis Sánchez and Messi. It was the fourth game they had played away from home where they hadn't played their first-choice starting eleven. David Villa was on the bench again.

Although Real Madrid went ahead after twenty-two seconds following a gift from Víctor Valdés to Ángel Di María that enabled Benzema to score, Barça found a lifeline in two lapses in marking by Fabio Coentrao and in one deflected shot from Xavi to turn the game around and win 3-1.

However, this game again showed that despite the many midfielders who made up the starting eleven, Messi was still not playing close to the area; instead, Guardiola had him running from deep to try and actively participate in creating Barcelona's attacks. In practice, Barça didn't have a center forward, and the person who was closest to being one, David Villa, didn't operate as such when he played.

At that time, Barça needed to go forward with several players to cause danger against professional and packed defenses, because, as they had few attackers, these couldn't cope alone. The way Alexis scored against Real Madrid—receiving the ball from Messi in the final third of the pitch, bearing down on goal alone, and shooting from outside the area—was the exception to the rule.

For his two forwards to get into situations where they could shoot with their better foot, Guardiola was forced to put Alexis on the left, which was a position he found hard to get used to because he had always played on the right wing at Udinese. Messi didn't play as a box "9," so when Barça was up against an opponent who cleverly closed down the spaces at the back, they were stifled and couldn't find a way through.

To make matters worse, leaving Alexis so far forward was to take away one of his best-known strengths, that great ability he has for joining in with the defensive duties and contributing to decisive attacking transitions.

Guardiola was determined to make him resemble a number 9 as closely as possible, like the number on his back, but not at Udinese before, nor in Chile, nor at Arsenal afterward, had he done that, simply because that isn't his natural position, nor where his strengths can be best exploited. To make things worse, he had to get used to two of the most difficult tasks in the world: adapting to playing for Barça and with Messi.

A few days after that Real Madrid game, and although the result was favorable again, the Club World Cup final against Santos and a starting lineup featuring Busquets, Iniesta, Xavi, Thiago Alcántara, Fàbregas, and Messi showed that Guardiola was a long way from giving up on his determination not to attack with the same number of forwards he had used until the previous season. Although this was a final—a one-off game—it was highly unlikely that he would use that lineup any more than a couple of times again because of the impracticability it entailed. When opponents sit back and defend, even though you dominate possession, if you can't find the spaces, that possession becomes completely useless. In the end, you need different players, not more of the same. Guardiola likes to experiment, in this case with a double false 9, but even if he thinks the team played better than ever that season, the results and the lack of a trophy tell a different story.

The fact that that lineup secured victory at the Bernabéu—and that an even more radical one had done so against Santos—didn't mean that it always would. Guardiola used Messi and Alexis Sánchez alone up front when they visited Espanyol, another game which wasn't at all easy, and they dropped points again.

The Chilean continued to play on the left, staying out wide and waiting for the ball in order not to stray into Messi's area of influence; he played without pace, without bite, without a goal threat, while Messi and Iniesta were completely tied down by very alert and tight marking. Everyone knew the formula by now: "Everyone behind the ball, tie them down, and try and punish them on the break."

Barça went ahead with another headed goal from Fàbregas—he had scored another one at the Bernabéu a month before—but Espanyol didn't give them a second's peace and equalized in the eighty-fifth minute, although they could easily have done so long before that. This way was even worse because it left Barça with no time to react.

By then Guardiola had already taken Alexis off and replaced him with Pedro, whom he also put on the left, although as soon as Espanyol scored he moved him to the right.

In that game, Pep walked a tightrope; he played with the score, but he never tried to finish the game off. Just before Espanyol's goal, he had taken off Fàbregas and replaced him with Keita, a much more defensive midfielder.

The way he handled the emerging players was another point of contradiction in Guardiola's final season. In many away games, despite not having enough available forwards, he kept Isaac Cuenca and Christian Tello back, supposedly in order not to subject them to more pressure than they could handle. However, at the Camp Nou he used them relatively frequently.

When Barça had to go to Villarreal at the end of January, they did so without Iniesta, Villa, Alexis, or Pedro, all of whom were injured. Guardiola preferred to start with Busquets, Mascherano, Xavi, Fàbregas, Adriano, and Messi and left Cuenca and Tello on the bench. This game was one of the best examples of Guardiola combining his stubbornness in not trusting the forwards he had available—although they were the kids from the B team—and again not using his best weapons in a difficult away game.

Up to now, his wish to fill the midfield and for Cesc to function as the floating magical piece on the board hadn't worked. Barça's best games had been those where they had stuck to a 4–3–3, even though this had meant using Cuenca or Tello—or both. It was an incontrovertible truth.

Did Barça need Busquets and Mascherano in midfield against Villarreal? If you only have one forward on the pitch and Iniesta isn't there, then why not use Thiago Alcántara? That way they would have enjoyed better distribution of the ball, more creativity, and even more goal-scoring ability. That day, Barça was lacking all these things and ended up drawing 0-0.

After so many setbacks—many more than could be considered acceptable—Guardiola learned his lesson in the first leg of the Copa del Rey semi-final against Valencia at the Mestalla. In the previous round Barça had beaten Real Madrid at the Bernabéu, again with Busquets, Fàbregas, Xavi, and Iniesta in midfield; interestingly, Real Madrid were the only big team against whom not lining up with three natural attackers worked.

However, now, against Valencia, it was Messi, Cuenca, and Alexis Sánchez who started up front; although after sixty-three minutes, with the score 1-1, Dani Alves—who hadn't started—came on for the Chilean to play the last minutes as a winger.

It wasn't a typical Barça game, as they played to attack and let the opposition attack them to see who ended up hitting harder, instead of controlling events through dominating possession. Without Xavi and Iniesta, with Puyol playing at left back and Javier Mascherano in one of his first games at center back, Barcelona held on for a draw to leave the tie well poised for the return leg, where Guardiola played Messi, Cuenca, and Alexis Sánchez from the start, and they won 2-0.

However, on February 11, just three days after reaching the Copa del Rey final, Barça had a difficult away game at Osasuna, a side who hadn't lost at home in the first half of the season and who ended the season as the team with the third lowest number of games lost (ten), behind only Real Madrid and Barcelona.

Barça saw how Real Madrid had a comfortable lead of seven points in the league, a difference they needed to reduce. This was, literally, a life-or-death game for Guardiola.

In many previous away games Pep had refrained from using Cuenca and Tello when he didn't have other forwards because they were still too young to take on such a huge responsibility.

However, for this trip to Pamplona—an extreme situation, as Guardiola himself had admitted the night before—he decided to leave Xavi, Iniesta, and Fàbregas on the bench in order to rest them for the first leg of the last sixteen Champions League tie against Bayer Leverkusen. The solution? To hand a full debut to Sergi Roberto, who hadn't played a single minute in that league season, having only managed ninety in the whole of the previous season.

Which situation is more difficult? The seven points they needed to make up on Real Madrid in the league, or a game against a second-rung team in the Champions League?

That night, Pep's ideas, as well as the spirit and the creativity of Futbol Club Barcelona, were left like the pitch of the Kingdom of Navarra, frozen at minus three degrees. Barça had been slowly bleeding league points at all the difficult away grounds, and now their footballing anemia was finally confirmed. Barça lost against Osasuna, and Real Madrid accepted the invitation to extend their lead to ten points the following night at the Bernabéu against Levante.

In both the games against Valencia in the Copa del Rey mentioned previously, which were played just before that trip to Pamplona and where Barça played several reserves, it was obvious how much their identity and the dominance they had traditionally exerted on their opponents had been affected. At times, Valencia was very close to knocking them out, a clear sign that Guardiola should have picked up on to realize that he couldn't weaken his team with too many rotations in difficult games.

Fate was somewhat ironic against Osasuna because that day he did play with three forwards from the start, but this ended up weakening the make-up of a midfield that was already low on self-confidence and allowed a defensive horror show to make the title race an almost irrecoverably lost battle.

By way of a contrast, at all those grounds where Barça had dropped points, except at Villarreal, Real Madrid took all three points because Mourinho always started with his best players and was, above all else, pragmatic.

The final page in the story was written against Real Madrid at the Camp Nou. It was the last chance they had to pull off the miracle, to dream of winning the league after eleven victories in a row, following the defeat at Osasuna which had cut Real Madrid's lead to four points. If Barça were to win on that night, Saturday, April 21, 2012, it would leave the league up for grabs again with Real Madrid's lead down to one point with four games to play.

It was the most important week of the season, as so often happens in a short seven-day spell in April. Three days earlier, Barça had lost against Chelsea in the Champions League semi-final first leg, and to stay alive in both competitions they had no choice but to win two games in seventy-two hours. A very stiff challenge indeed.

Guardiola used Fàbregas the whole season as a sort of strange playmaker without the ball who wasn't the creative axis and who found it difficult to find a place on the pitch where he could feel really comfortable. So much so, that after three seasons he never did, and he ended up taking refuge in the call from Mourinho's Chelsea, where he would be able to play as he wanted and where his potential would be exploited.

Pep had put a lot of muddled effort into Cesc becoming defined as a center forward who would burst through the inside channels, but that only succeeded in bringing down his individual performances and those of the team to minimal levels. None of the formations where he used him as a fourth central midfielder gave better dividends than the 4–3–3.

April is the most sensitive month of the season, where not only physical condition counts, but also where the team is supposed to have reached a level of tactical maturity whereby the manager is able to choose the ideal formation for a decisive encounter, beyond the forced and recommended rotations he may be compelled to make.

For this life-or-death game against Real Madrid, Guardiola stretched the flexibility apparently offered by a team as tactically rich as Barça to breaking point and decided to try to surprise the opposition with an unexpected move, just as he had done two years before against Inter.

He set up with a three-man defense—Adriano, Mascherano, and Puyol. He put Alves on the right wing and populated the midfield again with Busquets—who was moved back to cover the space left by Alves—

Xavi, Thiago, and Iniesta. Tello was given the left wing while Messi was given freedom to play as a "10" far away from the penalty area.

Despite having so many creative, fast midfielders with so many well-learned habits, Messi was still participating too much in creating moves, and that was depriving Barça of having a player close to the opponents' penalty area capable of delivering a knockout blow. If Barça had had two other clearly defined forwards who could exploit the inside channels more, rather than the outside channels, it would have made more sense to have Messi a little farther from goal.

Guardiola gambled on Barça's prodigious recovery of the ball after they had lost it and their attacking possession indirectly putting Messi close to the opposition area, but that hardly happened because Real Madrid, faced with that lack of center forwards in the Catalan team, didn't sit back, instead playing with a very high back line. This carried a certain level of risk, but one part or another of the body had to remain uncovered. The blanket doesn't measure two meters, or, in this case, one hundred.

Real Madrid was lucky enough to find itself ahead after a fluky goal from a corner and painted the game a color that was too painful for Barça eyes. Xavi sometimes appeared like a second and sometimes like a first forward, while Messi never really found a position to hurt the very astute Real defense.

The experiment had failed again, but Guardiola took seventy minutes to try something different, or at least something more natural. He took Xavi off, put Alexis Sánchez on, and the Chilean equalized in the blink of an eye. It would be unfair to suggest that Alexis's goal—a point-blank shot into an empty net—came about because they had another much more attacking player up front, although there aren't many arguments against saying this either. The mere presence of another attacker pinned the center backs down, left more space for Messi between the defense and its midfielders, and the Argentinian threw himself like an arrow into that no-man's land to bring the move to fruition.

However, the euphoria from scoring the equalizer brought with it defensive distractions. All Barça's midfielders converged on the man on the ball, Mesut Özil, and an open road appeared through the middle that Ronaldo took advantage of to restore Real Madrid's lead. Now it was the Catalan team that suffered the effects of the short blanket.

The defeat by Real Madrid was a significant blow which was hard to take, because they hadn't seemed to know how to play, to play well, and to score goals. However, the many draws away from home during the season and the manner in which they were earned were even more painful.

Three days later, and still feeling the emotional effects of losing against Real Madrid, Barcelona faced their second key game against Chelsea. In the first leg Guardiola had played with the four midfielders; they lost 1-0, and this breathed life into a Chelsea side who had been suffering a big identity crisis since André Villas-Boas had taken over the team the previous summer and which had become more acute in the weeks leading up to the game following his sacking and the appointment of Roberto Di Matteo.

Again, Guardiola didn't go for a natural starting eleven and innovated again with three at the back, Puyol, Piqué, and Mascherano, Dani Alves on the bench, four in midfield, Busquets, Xavi, Fàbregas, and Iniesta, and three up front, Messi, Alexis, and Cuenca.

Chelsea didn't offer the same caliber of opposition as Real Madrid; they sat back and suffered the presence of the three forwards penetrating their box like arrows. To make matters worse, John Terry stupidly kicked Alexis Sánchez without the ball and was given a straight red card.

With all this playing in their favor and already 2-0 up, Barça's defense simply switched off and, unthinkably, Ramires scored from a situation very similar to that in which Cristiano Ronaldo had virtually won the league just a few nights before. A high defense, poor marking, and the invitation to score tamely past Víctor Valdés.

Would that goal have been scored if Guardiola had played a normal defense? Why leave out a player as important as Alves? Did Barça need to experiment like this to turn the 1-0 score line around against this Chelsea side? Would the first leg have finished with the same score line if Guardiola had played with three men up front? We'll never know the respective answers to these questions, but the most general moral of the story is that the path chosen by Pep wasn't the happiest one to continue his insatiable thirst for evolution, perfection, and trophies.

The second half was like again watching the game against Mourinho's Inter two years previously, although it left a worse taste in the mouth given the manifestly inferior quality of the opposition. That Inter team had a well-executed plan and believed in themselves, but this Chelsea team was only able to get a good result when their opponents allowed them to, but not entirely on their own.

It's no less true that Barça's luck was wearing a white shirt in the 2011-2012 season, as forty-four of their shots came back off the woodwork—fifteen of them from Messi.

Luck apart, Guardiola sees football as a science that is permanently in transition, changing, needing to evolve. And he's right, tactical stagnation only serves to impoverish a team—as it did with Vicente del Bosque's Spain—but the path he chose in his last season at Barça ended up being a step backwards compared to everything he had achieved before that in his burgeoning and brilliant career at the Camp Nou.

However, at Bayern Munich he explored completely different avenues. That Bayern was perfection personified in a football team, perhaps even more so than his own Barça team. From the moment he arrived at the Allianz Arena he was more innovative; he didn't overpopulate the midfield, instead making modifications that contributed to enhancing verticality and speed as alternatives to dominating possession, which was always non-negotiable.

Perhaps it was the most feasible option, because the team had Arjen Robben and Franck Ribéry, and he couldn't sideline them; instead, he needed to exploit their strengths. But in the following seasons he brought in more wingers, such as Douglas Costa and Kingsley Coman, although positionally dominating the midfield never stopped being a priority, as was shown with the arrival of Thiago Alcántara, Xabi Alonso, and Arturo Vidal, as well as the temporary conversion of Philipp Lahm to play there.

At Bayern, Guardiola continued his personal evolution as a manager and his insatiable search for perfection which he had started at Barça and which, to a certain point, he had slowed down himself with his formations in his last season at the Camp Nou. In Munich he became more pragmatic, more flexible, and less fanciful. He tried several distinct formations, all of which worked well. He wasn't so obsessive about possession for possession's sake, but took advantage of a more direct attacking style and continued to demand and get the same levels of recovery of the ball when it was lost.

Moving Lahm to midfield, something which came about due to a temporary need in the 2013 UEFA Super Cup against Chelsea, was one of those points chosen by Pep to internally evolve the side and motivate his players to always remain tactically alert. He could allow himself the luxury of doing this because of the quality of Lahm, because it helped him to ensure the ball was brought out of defense safely, and because at the end of the day Bayern only had to defend very occasionally.

Leaving aside the little opposition they faced in his three seasons at the Allianz Arena, that Bayern side worked like clockwork finely tuned down to the last thousandth of a second, and this had a lot to do with the lessons Guardiola had learned from paths he mistakenly took in the last of his four years at Barça.

Interestingly, that great Bayern Munich team was never able to get past the semi-final stage of the Champions League because differences are greatly reduced when everything is decided over two matches. Fortunately, no team can attack mercilessly and be immune to what the opposition does. There's always an antidote to any poison. If you're a possession-based team, you're vulnerable to counterattacks. If you're a team that sits back and defends, you'll find it hard to score. If a side bases its game on the amount of possession it has, then it'll find it hard when the opposition fights for possession and shuts off possible passes.

Although perfect, Guardiola's Bayern weren't infallible. Real Madrid and Atlético de Madrid, with different weapons to those of Bayern and to each other, brought these to bear to snatch European glory away from them. That's why no system, however dominant it may be at any given time, can be sure of being effective forever. It's impossible to produce generation after generation of players with the same philosophy who enjoy the same success. Something will have to change, sooner rather than later.

Chapter 6

MOURINHO'S REAL MADRID—TWO OF A KIND

The 2010 World Cup worked its magic on certain rich clubs in Europe, who rushed to swell the size of their squads. At Real Madrid they paid more attention to what was going on in South Africa than in the European leagues, because their main signings were basically players who excelled there.

After spending nearly 200 million Euros (approximately 228 million dollars) the previous summer, the Bernabéu opened its doors to Mesut Özil, Ángel Di María, and Sami Khedira, all of whom performed excellently at the World Cup, as well as Ricardo Carvalho, Pedro León, and Sergio Canales, the latter having been "tied down" a year before but then continuing to play at Racing Santander in a display of high-handedness by a Real Madrid who wanted to get hold of any promising young players to emerge in Spain who weren't in the Barça academy. All so that he could play 282 minutes in the whole season and end up going to Valencia on loan.

But none of these contradictions was as dramatic as the arrival of the man who was destined to transform Real Madrid into a winning team, someone who was arriving at the pinnacle of his career after winning the treble with Inter—though not without a big scare in Serie A—and who vowed to shake up the hierarchy imposed by Barcelona in the Spanish league.

José Mourinho had actually just knocked Barça out of the Champions League and offered that psychological boost together with mental warfare, a combination which at first was absorbed by the ambition to win held by all parties involved, but which over time became as unsustainable as it was devastating.

"Let's see, who are people saying is the best manager in the world—Mourinho? Ah, well let's bring him here then. It doesn't matter how much it costs. If the check has the Real Madrid logo on it, he is sure to come," was the view taken by Jorge Valdano and Florentino Pérez. But three years later the talk had turned and was as contrary as Mourinho's personality.

How Manuel Pellegrini had done in his first season didn't matter. It didn't matter that the Chilean had been ushered in with much fanfare just one year before during Florentino's presidential campaign. That's all it was: fanfare. The probationary period offered by Real Madrid is so slim that even managers and people as exceptional as Carlo Ancelotti have been shown the door after a trophy-less season.

The image of the club, flitting from flower to flower, year after year, to see where the best pollen is, seems to matter little. "And he's given Barça some good hidings! That's our man!"

The previous season at Inter, Mourinho ended up playing with Sneijder and three forwards and winning the treble. Real Madrid is a team where you're obliged to play attractive, attacking football and appease both the scoreboard and the fans. You can't be excessively pragmatic because you have to give your players freedom so that trophies can be won playing an attractive brand of football. After all, all those millions are spent for a reason, aren't they?

In his first weeks, Mourinho tried out all the players he had in the squad until he settled on his best eleven with Özil, Ronaldo, Di María, and Higuaín up front and Xabi Alonso and Khedira as his regular holding midfielders. A balanced but attacking formation, exactly what Real Madrid should play with, a replica of his starting eleven at Inter.

But Higuaín was struck down by his herniated disc at the end of November, and Real Madrid found itself in a very difficult situation in mid-season, when signing a world-class forward who was eligible to play in the Champions League was almost impossible. On the bench was Benzema, who at that time was playing badly and had a poor goal-scoring record.

Even though Mourinho had officially arrived in the summer, it was on November 29 that he really landed in Spain. On that day, at the Camp Nou, he played his first proper game in La Liga, his real welcome.

Although Mourinho remained faithful to his formation and just made the forced change of Benzema for Higuaín, on that day Barça played with the ball and with Real Madrid. Mourinho knew that they were going to have little time with the ball and few chances, but although he faced an entirely expected scenario, there was never the tactical organization his players had shown in all the games they had played up to that point.

For the second half, with his team down 2-0and having floated like a ghost around the pitch, Mourinho put Lassana Diarra on for Mesut Özil. He must have thought that if it was impossible to contain Barça, get the ball, and launch an organized attack with his initial approach, now, at least, they would be able to achieve the first of these things, even though he knew the game was already up. It was considered quite normal to lose 2-0 to that Barça side.

On that day, the attack-minded Mourinho, the Mourinho who solved problems logically and by playing good football, vanished into thin air. Now he wanted Real Madrid to play long balls, to play too vertically and too quickly, attacking blindly. In 90 percent of cases these actions didn't lead to anything. How did Mourinho not notice this? Not when the score was 1-0, nor when it was 2-0. Never. The Real Madrid players were extras in a film which only had protagonists and which ended in a 5-0 thrashing.

When he faced the press, Mourinho said:

> *Humiliation? No, not at all. It is the biggest defeat in my career; I have never lost 5-0 before. But it is a defeat which is easy to digest; it is a defeat without chances to win. It is not one of those defeats where you are left with a taste which is difficult to accept because you didn't deserve to lose or you have lost because the referee made a decision which influenced the result, or because you have hit the post two or three times and you lose because of bad luck.*

And he added:

> *It is not like that at all. One team played to the maximum of their potential and the other team played very badly; the result does not change anything at all. It is a well-deserved victory and a well-deserved defeat and that is why it is easy to digest.*[29]

With these words Mourinho was just trying to hide the true consequences that this game had for his players and for himself. A score of 5-0 hurts you and drives you crazy. That night marked a before and after in Real Madrid's aspirations to win the league because it had become clear that Barça's lead was impossible to reduce in the head-to-head games and that they would depend on the other teams in the league to bring them level.

The next game, at home to Valencia, laid bare the gaping wounds from the previous Monday's trip to the Camp Nou. Mourinho started with a surprising central triumvirate—the one which he had used in the second half against Barça—but this time the player sacrificed wasn't Özil, but Benzema.

But after reaching half-time at 0-0, he had no choice but to go back to the natural 4–4–2, and after nine minutes of the second half he took Khedira off and put Benzema on. Valencia's David Albelda was sent off after sixty-five minutes for a very dubious handball, and that was when Real Madrid found more space to launch their counterattacks, because Valencia never sat back to try and hold out for a draw.

Cristiano Ronaldo managed to find a corridor of space to score the opening goal after seventy-three minutes, which instead of calming Mourinho served to stir his inner fears, and he immediately replaced Özil with Esteban Granero. Even later, and still winning 1-0, he took Di María off and shored up the midfield still further with Mahamadou Diarra.

Ronaldo scored again from a similar situation to his first—a swift counter after the ball was won in the center circle—and with three minutes remaining Real Madrid sealed victory after spending almost the entire game very nervous and cautious.

"I showed that I respected Valencia by putting out a team which gave more stability. This was not a day for playing a great game or scoring a

lot of goals," said Mourinho in order to justify the lineup he had chosen, although he did also say that his formation was due more to the effects the 5-0 at the Camp Nou had had than the actual opposition they were facing against Valencia.[30]

Mourinho revealed that his players' self-confidence had taken a blow after their trip to Barcelona and that he needed stability in midfield to avoid conceding a goal in the opening minutes, as that would have been a blow which would have been difficult for his players to recover from.

However, in La Liga there was no other team capable of joining battle with the big two, and the leaders didn't drop too many points along the way. Barça didn't drop their pace, and Real Madrid kept going quietly along in second place as Mourinho's very offensive formation continued to bear fruit. In reality, apart from the games against Barça, there wasn't too much to worry about. That was until the arrival of April, the great defining month.

Real Madrid reached the Champions League semi-finals, and it suddenly became clear that to win something—the league, Copa del Rey, or Champions League—they had to beat Barcelona on the way. Since January, they had both qualified for the final of the Copa del Rey, and the draw for the Champions League had thrown up two more "clásicos" at the semi-final stage. In all, there were to be four games against Barça in less than twenty days. One of those challenges would lead Mourinho to say to his inner circle: "*This is the type of thing I came here for*."

The league was already lost, but they still had to play the away game against Barça, and Mourinho decided to use that game as a laboratory for the lineup he would use four days later in the Copa del Rey final.

He used the central triumvirate again, surprising everyone by playing Pepe as the third man in midfield together with Xabi Alonso and Sami

Khedira—a position which wasn't entirely alien to him because he'd played there a few times for Portugal—leaving Mesut Özil out of the starting lineup and putting Ronaldo, Di María, and Benzema in attack.

That day, besides the positive tactical result he was able to claim with that wall in midfield, there was something much more important at play, something which would allow him to come to the two cup ties, which were after all the most relevant three games of the four, at less of a disadvantage. That day, Real Madrid needed not to lose so that their players didn't feel psychologically inferior and Barça didn't feel even more dominant than they already were.

And they managed it, despite playing with ten men from the fifty-second minute and conceding a penalty which Messi converted. Real Madrid never gave up; they went full out in search of the equalizer and got it after a very dubious foul on Marcelo which the referee gave a penalty for. The way the Brazilian full back celebrated the penalty award is enough to give cause for further doubt about whether a foul had actually been committed. The person who did manage to see the real significance of the award was Mourinho, as it meant that they had come back in front of their own fans to level the game. It was exactly what he had wished for, and he'd gotten his own way, regardless of how.

In the Copa del Rey final he repeated the same formation and emerged victorious because the feeling that everything is decided in a one-off game reduces differences, because every minute that passed without the stalemate being broken moved Real Madrid closer to Barça's level—that night—and because it was all he could do, because if Real Madrid had tried to go toe to toe with Barça, they would have been eaten alive.

At no point did Mourinho decide to go with the same attacking formation that he'd used for the whole season and with which his team had felt so comfortable. He had already forgotten how important it was to keep the fans happy and to move forward in what, in the long run, would be the most suitable and sensible direction. Barça is different, we all know that, but was this not just a way to avoid the real solution? Did he need to change so much just to play a single opponent? If he had won everything the previous year with a really attacking formation and had even managed to beat Barça like that, why not try the same thing now?

Mourinho was a type of Dr. Jekyll the previous season and a Mr. Hyde this season. The 5-0 against Barça in November was the potion for his metamorphosis. One game. Now the experiment was going well for him. At the very least it was justified.

But the Champions League semi-finals were approaching, and they had to play the first leg at home. Fate laid before him a difficult and critical decision. If the first leg had been away, it would have been clear and to a certain point understandable that they should defend with everything, try and get the best result possible, and then go out and try and win the tie in their own stadium with a little more freedom.

But no, the return leg would be at the Camp Nou, and they needed to be prepared for the worst. They couldn't go to Barcelona with the tie already out of reach because it was very unlikely they could turn it around on their enemy's patch. Mourinho had no choice but to repeat what he'd done a year before with Inter, where the key to their qualification for the final was the result gained in Milan, a 3-1 win, which Barça, even with a man extra in the return leg, couldn't turn around.

But instead what did we find? That he set up in the Santiago Bernabéu with the same formation he used in the Copa del Rey final, which didn't offer even the slimmest chance of surviving the storm that would break over them a week later. Indeed, it gave no guarantee of getting the result needed that night. They needed goals to counterbalance the ones they would surely concede in the return leg. It was no good repeating the approach adopted for the final of the Copa del Rey, where they only scored one goal, and that in extra time. It was no good clinging to a thread dangling from a dead branch.

In the book *Why So Many Victories?*, Mourinho says that "*the most important thing in a team is to have a defined model, defined principles, to know them well, to interpret them well, regardless of whether you use this player or that one. At the end of the day that is what I call game organization.*"[31] This is the basis of tactical periodization, his favorite training method, which he inherited from his teacher Vitór Frade and which responds completely to the playing philosophy he wishes to impose on the pitch.

So why break with his model and his principles? Those principles he calls key to game organization and whose interpretation, starting with training, is his path to success. Why play differently now to the style he had inculcated in his players since he had arrived? Isn't the best way to continue on the road to glory perhaps applying the method that has brought the most success so far?

It wasn't necessary to wait until the end of the game to predict that Real Madrid's fate in the Champions League was sealed the moment those eleven players stepped onto the pitch. They lost 0-2 and paved the way for Barça to win their second Champions League trophy in three years.

Putting aside Pepe's red card—questionable, and one which the German referee should never have shown him because the situation favored Barça again and added fuel to Mourinho's excuses—Real Madrid never found the way to get what they needed.

Mourinho's capacity to interpret and read the game, and the wisdom to know that not all games or cup ties can be prepared for in the same way, failed him. We come back again to the omnipresent theme of evolution, although in this case it's more a question of common sense, logic, and allowing the footballers to be the main players in the whole spectacle.

Mourinho, from his position pitch side, seeks to have too much influence on what happens on the pitch, but when you try to squeeze out so much fluency and tie down your players so much, you'll only succeed in limiting their performance and putting an end to the progression you may have achieved up to that point.

His own ambition and self-confidence sometimes end up betraying him, and this Barça, which was almost perfect, left very little room for error. They might be beaten once, like in the Copa del Rey final, but to manage it consistently Mourinho needed to use a less flimsy, less passive method that would allow his own players to be able to exploit their strengths.

But in a way this was a step forward—at least quantitatively—against the dominance Barça had exerted on Real Madrid in the three preceding seasons, including this one. Winning a trophy and defeating the all-powerful Catalan side in a final laid the groundwork for continuing to try to knock down the wall the following season. Very soon, Mourinho was going to let us see how valuable it was to him to learn from his own mistakes.

In his second season at the Santiago Bernabéu, Mourinho and Real Madrid benefited from the constant draws Barça notched up in the league, and they had a very easy ride almost all the way. Indeed, when things were getting very tense with five games left to play and needing to travel to the Camp Nou, Real Madrid ended up winning 2-1 and settling the league title.

This comfort allowed Mourinho to cling to the same attacking formation he had consolidated in his first year—except in the games against

Barça—and Real Madrid ended up securing 100 points and scoring 121 goals. It's true that these figures aren't entirely convincing evidence of the team's goal-scoring threat, since the difference at that time between Real Madrid and Barcelona and the other teams in La Liga was practically the same as that between the first and second division in any league, but Real Madrid managed to put a stop to Barça's supremacy and ended up hastening the departure of Guardiola from Camp Nou.

Despite having beaten Barcelona in the endurance race that is the league, in six games against Pep that 2011-2012 season—two in the Spanish Super Cup, two in the Copa del Rey, and two in the league—Real Madrid only won once and were beaten in the first two competitions.

However, Mourinho never put a third "destroyer" in midfield again, instead putting confidence in his four forwards, Özil, Di María, Ronaldo, and Benzema. With a clearly defined 4–2–3–1, they lost twice to Barça in the Santiago Bernabéu in a little over a month—first in the league and then in the Copa del Rey—but this didn't change his ideas, and when he had to play the key second league game at the Camp Nou, he kept to the same lineup he had used all season, and he effectively won the league.

Once again there was evolution, and it ended up bearing fruit, although particularly against Barça the balance wasn't positive. In the last four seasons, including the last two with Mourinho, Real Madrid had played fifteen times against Barcelona and had only won twice.

Strangely, that league title decider on April 21 in Barcelona was sandwiched between the two Champions League games against Bayern Munich. Real Madrid lost 2-1 in the first leg at the Allianz Arena, while the reverse score line in the return leg in the Bernabéu forced extra time and penalties, which led to the German team qualifying for the final.

These two games against Bayern and the six against Barça were the only ones against really strong opposition that Real Madrid had to play all season, which, to a large extent, contributed to Mourinho not being able to perfect the great attacking machinery he had built, which was ineffective against powerful opponents.

The return leg against Bayern showed that Real Madrid was missing that bit of ruthlessness and the X factor needed to overcome an opponent of the same stature. After fourteen minutes they were winning 2-0 and felt in control psychologically, but the German side didn't lose their cool, managed to level the tie after twenty-eight minutes, and little by little levelled the mental battle until they got to penalties, without Mourinho and his side being able to finish them off before then.

It was a hard blow for the Portuguese manager because they had taken a healthy lead in the blink of an eye but been unable to protect it. Part of the blame for that failure lies squarely with him because he was unable to transmit to his players how to manage the situation successfully.

So, after a season of contrasts, but with the significant boost to morale provided by winning the league and knocking Barcelona off their perch, Mourinho set off on what would turn out to be his last season at the Santiago Bernabéu. The last chapter gave him some very toxic months, both on a footballing and a personal level, which finished with the disintegration of the team and where Mourinho showed his lack of humility and emotional intelligence in facing adverse situations that every manager and every team have to face with greater or lesser frequency.

However, he was able to find Barcelona's weak points to the extent that in the clásicos he lost just one game in six—the first leg of the Spanish Super Cup—exactly the opposite of the previous season.

Mourinho pressed very high when Barça tried to bring the ball out, with speed in both transitions, coherently, and with a defensive solidity unseen in more than three years against the Catalan team. But why did this high line not work in the 5-0 game and then did after that? Because when Barça plays 4–3–3, even though Messi plays farther back, there are still two wide attackers who burst through like arrows, exploit the channels between the center backs and the full backs, and are difficult to mark. When Barça changed to play with just two up front and Messi moved away from the penalty area, it was easier to neutralize the lone attacker who was left up front. Unless there are individual mistakes, like the one where Alexis Sánchez lost his marker in the 1-3 at the Bernabéu in December 2011 in the league, the high line isn't so risky if it's carried out well.

But for all that the power in "the mother of all matches" swung toward Real Madrid, the bad atmosphere in the dressing room, the deterioration of Mourinho's relationship with the players, the illogical relegation of Casillas to the bench, and the lead Barça opened up very early on in the league all made it impossible for him to retain his ties with Real Madrid.

At the start of the season, after two defeats and a draw in the first four league games, Mourinho felt that he didn't have a team, and he said so publicly. "*There are few committed and focused heads. Few players now believe that football is the center of their lives. And it is my fault. At half-time I took two players off, but I wanted to take seven off,*" he said after the defeat against Sevilla and a few days before the home game against Manchester City in the first Champions League match.[32]

And he added: "*My team worries me, not the points difference. It worries me because since the official season started we have only played [well] in the Super Cup. No more. Not at all against Getafe and Sevilla, little against Valencia, very little against Granada. More than the points, what worries me is that at the moment I do not have a team.*" At that time, the star of the team was better known as Tristiano ["sad Cristiano"].

Obviously Mourinho wasn't the only one at fault in this strange debacle; the players' individual errors and, in his words, "*the image of a team without focus, without the mental disposition for suffering*," who work non-stop on set pieces only to concede a goal from a corner in the first minute, were also to blame.

Against Manchester City in the Champions League he decided to change things at a stroke. He went back to the three holding midfielders and no playmaker. No Özil, no Kaká, no Modrić, all of whom started on the bench. Now Real Madrid was reduced to a Ronaldo-long-shot-dependence, which led to them going behind, although they managed to come back more through grit and determination than good football.

They got through the Champions League group phase, although not without a fight, in second place after Borussia Dortmund, but the league was all but lost because Barça won eighteen out of nineteen games in the first half of the season. Real Madrid was therefore left with its players' and manager's continuing thirst for trophies, which, in the case of competitions with shorter phases of two-legged ties like the Champions League and the Copa del Rey, might be enough to lift a cup. That's how unfair football is at times.

Mourinho's relationship with his players had been breaking down for some time. The team was finding it difficult to score from situations other than set pieces, crosses, or counterattacks, and the players were beginning to question the ability of Mourinho, who in the defeat against Betis ended up playing with Sergio Ramos as a center forward. He also started his crusade against the referees to try and justify the team's poor results.

Mourinho had a feeling that all the revolutions he had caused could end up getting him the sack, but even so he didn't shy away from fronting up to the situation by requesting all possible power. Although Jorge Valdano left his post as sporting director and Florentino Pérez gave full powers to Mourinho, his command of the dressing room and his affinity with the squad's heavyweights were not total, and he never kept the control he had exercised in his previous stints at Chelsea and Inter Milan.

Relegating Casillas to the bench was a way to try and show who was boss in the dressing room against the growing internal instability of the team, a completely false move that actually showed clearly that Mourinho didn't see himself still on the bench beyond the summer.

In the Champions League, the draw for the last sixteen pitted them against a Manchester United side which was solid in the Premier League but had weaknesses that could be exploited. After a very even first leg where Real Madrid just about managed to draw at home, Nani's red card at Old Trafford shifted the tie inexorably in Real Madrid's favor. But when both teams played with eleven men, Real Madrid was no better than United.

After beating Galatasaray without too many problems in the quarter-finals, the semi-final against Borussia Dortmund looked a bit more difficult; they had already come up against the German side in the group stage and hadn't been able to beat them in either game.

Di María was given special permission to join the squad late before the first leg due to the premature birth of his daughter. In his place Mourinho started with Luka Modrić, who joined Xabi Alonso and Sami Khedira in midfield, changing his usual 4–2–3–1 formation. Real Madrid then tried to send balls into the box from the wings, again and again, which resulted in abysmal failure, and didn't try to apply a shred of quality to the possession they had.

Plan (?) A didn't work. Play didn't go through the feet of either Modrić or Özil, even though these two players had given ample evidence that they knew how to set the tempo for a game, but at that moment they weren't soloists but members of an out-of-tune orchestra who didn't follow their timing, and they, logically, couldn't play all the instruments. Dortmund's blistering speed swept them aside, and when Real Madrid had the ball we were made to wonder what the point was of having Modrić and Özil on the pitch.

The Real Madrid defense that day had one of their worst games in recent history and showed a great naivety in not anticipating that the balls played through could end up with any of the German team's agile forwards. A number 9 as lethal as Robert Lewandowski can't be given the tiniest of spaces, but that day the Pole had the time of his life, scoring four times and causing the justified fury of Mourinho toward his defenders, although we should also ask ourselves where his capacity for foreseeing events and producing a coherent plan to minimize Dortmund's offensive threat and avoid such a tactical dismantling was.

While it was the defensive errors that did for Real Madrid in the first leg, their imprecise passing and excessive and desperate verticality in the return leg stopped them from mounting a comeback. They ended up scoring two goals toward the end of the game, but the third one didn't arrive, and Borussia Dortmund went through to the Champions League final. For Real Madrid, another road to the décima (tenth Champions League title), one of the main objectives Mourinho was brought to the Santiago Bernabéu to achieve, was shut off, and the back door of the institution was beginning to open for him to leave by.

He had probably agreed his return to Chelsea a long time beforehand, because he already felt on his way out of Real Madrid. Relations between him and his players had broken down and so, while sometimes a couple of good games may be enough to win a trophy, Real Madrid was so devoid of anything that they found it impossible to overcome an opponent that functioned—from the most general perspective—as a team.

Life was fair, and Mourinho left Madrid empty-handed in his last season, sent off in the Copa del Rey final at the Santiago Bernabéu while the players he'd managed up to that day fell at the hands of Atlético de Madrid in extra time. This was merely the image of what Mourinho had caused with his rebelliousness, his intolerance, and his immaturity when he was unable to manage something as common in football as losing. Mourinho doesn't know how to deal with bad results; he gets confused, he goes crazy, and while he was able to lift trophies at all the clubs he has managed, his departure at the end of his two spells at Chelsea and his time at Real Madrid came about in very unpleasant circumstances and with the dressing room in flames. Mourinho has two very different sides to him, and the club which is attracted to the brilliant side also inevitably ends up buying the sick side as well. It's just a question of time before it ends up exploding.

That Real Madrid side got weaker every year, despite having one of the strongest squads and one of the most successful managers in the world. However, his capacity to handle the inevitable setbacks any team will suffer was, however, in doubt again. A manager must know not only how to build success, but also how to save the boat from sinking when the storm breaks and minimize the damage in order to be able to sail in calmer waters again. Anybody can have a bad season; it's not degrading to go a year without winning a trophy, although at Real Madrid this is seen as an inadmissible sin.

After the defeat by Borussia Dortmund in the Champions League semi-final, Mourinho blurted out that before he'd arrived at Real Madrid the club had had eighteen managers in twenty-one years and had only reached the European Cup/Champions League semi-final on five occasions, but with him they had reached it in all three seasons.

But nobody reminded him that before 1997 you had to be league champions to play in the European Cup; in other words, Real Madrid wouldn't have been in a position to qualify for the tournament in all the seasons mentioned by Mourinho. If there's nothing to grab hold of, there just isn't—it's as simple as that.

The day Real Madrid lost the Cup final against Atlético, he did attend the press conference, but on countless occasions it was Aitor Karanka, his assistant, who faced the media, because when things go badly, Mourinho doesn't like being asked probing questions that might leave him looking bad.

Everybody reaped what they had sown. The club and Florentino believed that "Mourinho was the best manager in the world," as if such a thing existed, and trusted that "he was what they needed to defeat Barça." They didn't look at the dark side of a moon that was not only shining but also waning. They didn't consider that after a couple of years of potential glory the hell of the third season could arrive, as had been the norm at his previous clubs. They didn't notice that the atmosphere Mourinho creates is so unsustainable that it ends up reaching dimensions similar to those of his ability to win trophies.

Interestingly, that season he did manage to overcome Barça in their head-to-head meetings—he won three out of six and only lost one—which was the only consolation he was able to walk away from the Santiago Bernabéu for good with.

Chapter 7

MOURINHO'S RETURN TO ENGLAND AND THE SEARCH FOR THE RIGHT WAY

Many players have mentioned Mourinho's unrivalled capacity to motivate and get the best out of every player by focusing on the psychological side of the game. In his last season at Real Madrid that motivation reached a point where it was so toxic and aggressive that it started to produce exactly the opposite effect. The players started performing below their ability level, and the team lost that privileged position where Mourinho puts it above any individual.

In the book, *José Mourinho: Special Leadership*, the Portuguese writer Luis Lourenço admits that he was obsessed with finding out how Mourinho would react after a big defeat. At the time that he was so absorbed with finding the answer, Chelsea had won twice in a row in the Premier League and was involved in a close title race with Manchester United in the 2006-2007 season.

Lourenço couldn't contain himself any longer, and he ended up asking Mourinho his million-dollar question. "*Normal*," Mourinho replied. "*It will be like with everyone else. I know I will lose one day and I'm prepared for it, so I don't even think about it. When it happens I'll be here to face the consequences that a defeat always brings. However, I don't think it will be anything special in terms of attitude or reaction*," he added.[33]

Reality has shown us that Mourinho doesn't like losing and that he finds it hard to keep his composure when it happens. Every time a team of his goes through a bad spell, it consumes him, and he's unable to find a way out of it. He can no longer say that he's not used to defeats—as he did in that famous press conference when he called Arsène Wenger a "*specialist in failure*"—because he's now experienced it fairly frequently. It can't be denied that in many of his clubs he's worked under great pressure and that there's no room for failure, but Mourinho is a catalyst for his own sacking when his teams become divorced from the winning path.

In his first spell at Chelsea he didn't get to the end of September in his fourth season; Real Madrid came completely off the rails in his third season, and he didn't start the next one (and he may only have stayed to the end of the third season because he got to the Champions League semi-final and the Copa del Rey final), while in his second spell at Chelsea he left in December of his third year. It remains to be seen how long the honeymoon lasts at Manchester United. In all these cases he had won trophies in each of the preceding seasons, but the upheaval was so unbearable that his winning record counted for nothing.

This trend tells us that things go well for Mourinho as long as his teams are performing well, but that he hasn't shown himself to be very skilled in getting them out of the inevitable slumps in which teams will find themselves in any of the competitive leagues where he's managed so far. Leaving Real Madrid in the way he did left him bitter, angry, and too furious to be cool-headed enough to face his new spell at Chelsea.

Although he may try to deny it, deep down he knows this, and it eats away at him.

In order to try to raise his self-esteem a little after leaving the Santiago Bernabéu, Mourinho made it known that he felt that Chelsea needed him, although he didn't want his words to be taken as a lack of modesty on his part. He also said that it would have been an easy decision to have gone to a less competitive league—perhaps referring to Carlo Ancelotti and Paris Saint-Germain—but that he had come to a competition and a club where it wasn't easy to win the league. This depends on how you look at it, as it would be interesting to know the competitiveness analysis the Sunderland, Atalanta, or Espanyol managers' would have done.

After losing away to Everton in the fourth game of the 2013-2014 Premier League season, Mourinho said that he was aiming to transform his players—or, in his exact words, "*beautiful young eggs*"—into serious contenders for the league title.

They were, "*eggs that need a Mum, in this case … a Dad, to take care of them, to keep them warm during the winter, to bring the blanket and work and improve them. One day the moment will arrive when the weather changes, the sun rises, you break the eggs and the eggs are ready to go for life at the top level,*" he said.[34]

But it seems that these eggs were still a long way from maturing, because four days later his innocent chicks lost to Basel at Stamford Bridge in the Champions League, after which he took the same view again.

"*The team probably is not a team with such maturity and personality to face the difficult moments of the game,*" he said. He spoke specifically about Samuel Eto'o, to whom he had given a season-long contract. "*Samuel, maybe, lacks sharpness, but this is something that doesn't surprise me because, when you are two and a half years at a place that doesn't motivate you* [he had been lured to Anzhi Makachakla by a very juicy contract], *off the main stage, and maybe you are there not for the right reasons, you lose the hunger, your appetite*."[35] This might cause us to wonder whether that was something he was expecting, why he had signed him, and why he had started him in that game.

Jamie Redknapp, working for *Sky Sports*, confirmed the feeling that after a month of the official season, it was impossible to make out a half-visible tactical coherence. "*If it wasn't José Mourinho, you'd probably be thinking 'What is this guy up to? What's their best system? What's their identity? How do they play?' I've seen him from the start of the season use so many players in different positions*," he said.

He also referred to what seemed the biggest surprise. "*No Mata. I still can't believe why he doesn't pick him. When I'm thinking about Chelsea retaining the ball, people comfortable on it, he has to play*."

And he finished: "*I don't think José really knows what his best team is. When you play football, it's about building relationships – be it centre backs, midfielders, wide men, front men. At the moment, no one seems to have any relationship with anyone because they don't know who he is going to play*."[36]

This only goes to show that Mourinho didn't manage a calmer, less stormy, less stressful start to his second spell at Chelsea, without as much upheaval or despair. Football is often a case of more haste less speed, and for the shell to break at just the right time, the most important qualities are often patience and calmness.

In the goalless draw at Old Trafford in the third game of the league season, Mourinho played André Schürrle as a lone striker, despite the fact that he wasn't used to playing in that position. But this was a game where it was more important to him not to lose. Days later, in the defeats against Everton and Basel, he used Samuel Eto'o to spearhead the attack.

If Mourinho had started watching the Chelsea matches the moment he knew he would be going back to Stamford Bridge, he would have noticed that central defense was one of the most critical areas of the team and that central attack also needed a lot of attention. He might have found a way to get Mata and Oscar to work together and realized that it wasn't necessary to shake everything up from the midfield forwards, which is what he finally ended up doing.

Before the match against Fulham, three days after the defeat against Basel, Mourinho revealed that the reason Mata wasn't his first choice as playmaker wasn't Mata himself, but the position to which Oscar was relegated as a result.

He argued:

> *It is one thing to play with Ramires and Oscar closing down opponents on each side, and Mata as a No. 10 behind a striker with his clever assists, clever passes and fantastic actions because he has great talent. But it is another thing to adapt to the way we want [or I want?] to play. I'm not ready to ask Oscar to track opposing full backs. I want to build with Oscar as my No. 10. I want the other two players, from the side, to adapt to that reality and learn how to do things they were not ready to do before.*
>
> *In this moment, Oscar is my No. 10 and, if anyone tells me Oscar has not been Chelsea's best player this season, I'd have to disagree.*[37]

The issue itself isn't that of the absence or not of Mata—although leaving him out might be considered highly unreasonable—or who should be given the playmaker role, but is rather Mourinho's own difficulty in coming to a decision on a stable and efficient starting lineup.

In the same interview where he had said that Chelsea needed him, Mourinho added that he would adapt to the qualities of the players at his disposal, but now he seemed to be proving exactly the opposite. He had a predetermined idea and he wanted his players to adapt to it.

Continuing his explanation about Oscar and Mata, he said:

> *Can they play together? Yes, they can. When he [Mata] adapts.*[37]

Whenever Mourinho has taken charge of a team it has never been his way to keep the same order of things which existed before his arrival. He's not a manager who is locked into a single formula, but he's also not someone who prefers a quiet transition. In this case he was even less likely to transition quietly, given that the man he had inherited the post from, Rafa Benítez, was one of the biggest rivals in his career.

On his return to Chelsea he wanted to make too many changes, and he didn't seem to have a coherent idea to justify such a revolution. There were things requiring special thought before being changed, like the importance of Mata, because of what he brought to the team and how comfortable and secure his teammates felt when he was on the pitch. Of course, Mata and Oscar could play together, and Ramires as well, forming a sort of diamond with John Obi Mikel as its defensive point, but Mourinho's own personal issues stopped him from trying this option.

After the two defeats against Everton and Basel, Chelsea saw the light with a victory at home against Fulham in the Premier League. After the game and when pressed on the subject by the media, Mourinho said that what he didn't like about Mata was his poor defensive work:

> *He has to be more consistent, has to participate more when the team loses the ball. It's not his fault, it's just the consequence of the way he has played in the last years. Since he arrived at Chelsea, the club has played very defensive football and with a low block all the time. The team was playing with two lines of four and playing counter-attacking football.*

And he left no doubts about the profound changes he wanted to implement at Chelsea:

> *Juan has fantastic quality and is very intelligent in the way he uses the ball. Now the situation is completely different.*[38]

Mourinho wanted his team to play high up the pitch and try to win the ball back quickly. He wanted to control games, to be active rather than reactive. He emphasized that in his first spell he had chosen to play long diagonal balls, but now he wanted to keep the ball on the ground more, to have faster movement, and to use possession in the right way.

Everything rested on the nature of the players he now had at his disposal, who had a different profile, which Mourinho had to adapt to and find a different way of playing. Mata, according to his philosophy, didn't offer a guarantee of correct defensive positioning once the team lost the ball.

However, the months passed and Chelsea lacked sustained periods of quality possession, although Mourinho persisted with his indefatigable search for it. What he was convinced of was that Mata wasn't going to be the key to unlock the change. Chelsea continued to be like throwing dice, where you never knew what number you would get. Mourinho was desperate to find an identity, but this was precisely the one thing that he didn't come across.

In December, after being knocked out of the League Cup by Sunderland after leading 1-0 until the eighty-eighth minute, and aware that his forwards weren't scoring a lot of goals, Mourinho moved on to a new phase, which he defined thus:

> *If I want to win 1-0 I think I can. I think it is one of the easiest things in football. You structure your team from the back, you organise your team from the defensive idea, you don't give freedom to your players to express themselves ... and what you do is you recover the ball and try to punish the opponent on the counter-attack.*

But he immediately dismissed—at least verbally—the idea that this was something he was considering implementing:

> *I don't want to because we are going in a direction which is the right direction in terms of the quality of football we want to play, and it's quite frustrating that you have to change that and go one step back and go in another direction just because you want better results. I don't want to do it.*[39]

If we read between the lines we can see that Mourinho was acknowledging his inability to put together a team that played "quality" football and got results. At the same time, the Chelsea defense was nowhere near solid enough to try and win games 1-0 either. The frequency with which his defenders made mistakes which cost goals and points was too high to consider trying it.

But to a certain extent he did start to apply a more defensive strategy, and against Arsenal at the Emirates Stadium on December 23, he did something he had rarely, and certainly not in the important games, done before that season: He put three men—Mikel, Lampard, and Ramires—in the center of midfield.

This wasn't counterproductive, because in practice it provided stability and balance to the midfield, while it allowed him to benefit from the two attacking midfielders joining the attack, but up until then he hadn't chosen to try it. The other surprise, perhaps a bigger one, was that Oscar was left on the bench. Up front were Hazard, Willian, and Fernando Torres.

The game was an extremely tight one with very few clear chances for either team. Both sides were very cautious, the battle was fierce in midfield, and there was little danger in either penalty area. Lampard and Ramires were given a lot more freedom as they played with Mikel behind them. This, obviously, was a weapon in Chelsea's favor. Arsenal had more possession, but the more dangerous moves were put together by Chelsea.

As the end of the game drew near, there was the feeling that, knowing the weaknesses of this Arsenal side, if Mourinho dared to push a little more, he could have gone away with all three points, which would have given Chelsea a tremendous boost, particularly in terms of morale.

But Mourinho was too cautious, not allowing Wenger's side the smallest hint of an advantage, but at the same time, as a logical consequence, denying his own side the same thing. He only made like-for-like substitutions: Schürrle for Hazard and Oscar for Willian—being rather kind with the term "like-for-like" in the case of the latter—and finished it off by replacing Fernando Torres with David Luiz three minutes from time.

If we want to find something positive in this approach, we can say that at least he saved his team from any psychological blows. A defeat would have given Arsenal a huge lift and would have been an enormous step backward in Chelsea's consolidation. It kept them on that upward curve which would then soar with the victories against Swansea, Liverpool, and Southampton in the busy schedule of Christmas fixtures.

After the Arsenal game, Mourinho defended his team's approach, saying: "*When we wanted, we let them have the ball more and we looked after our defence. We had the game completely under control. It was very important not to lose*."[40] Perhaps the most important thing.

Things started to change toward the end of December. Chelsea started to show some intent in their play; the defense—with Terry and Ivanović spearheading it—became more solid, while Oscar emerged as the midfield axis and Hazard was the most influential of his forwards given the lack of goals—but not of mobility and influence—of Fernando Torres.

The attacking midfielders started to provide excellent cover for the full backs; they ran back, they pressed, they marked. Chelsea changed into a compact, structured team whose players were no longer isolated pieces but were now closely connected to each other, both in footballing terms and mentally.

Despite not having a construction as elegantly assembled as Arsenal and Manchester City, Chelsea cavorted with risk and took advantage of the slightest chink in their opponent's armory. Arsenal, Liverpool, Swansea, and Southampton, four of the most effective teams in the Premier League that season, could do nothing against them. This was a Chelsea which fed more and more on possession, so much so that they instinctively pounced to recover it when they lost it. Against Liverpool, in the ninetieth minute, they were pressing in their opponents' area to stop them bringing the ball out.

Before the year had ended, Chelsea hadn't lost to any of the big clubs and had beaten Liverpool and Manchester City at home and drawn away to Manchester United and Arsenal. This could be seen as a good sign, but the same thing was happening as had happened the previous season with Mourinho's Real Madrid when they had beaten Barça in the Spanish Super Cup, knocked them out of the Copa del Rey, and not lost to them in both league games but had dropped too many points against weaker league opposition.

The game against Southampton on the first day of 2014 showed that Mourinho was right, in a way, about Mata. At that time, games were coming thick and fast, and he needed to rest players. For that difficult away game at the St Mary's, he started with Mata and Schürrle up front with Hazard and Torres, while he left Oscar and Willian on the bench.

Southampton had more possession and that meant Chelsea's defense and defensive midfield—with the essential support of Hazard and Schürrle—had a very tense afternoon. Chelsea, meanwhile, saw little of the ball and had virtually no quality possession, which contributed to Mata, a player who becomes useless without the ball, not feeling comfortable on the pitch.

After fifty-three minutes, Mourinho took off Schürrle and Mata, who was visibly furious when he got to the bench, and put on Willian and Oscar. In just a few minutes these two had contrived to make the score 3-0 with relative ease, as if to suggest that if almost an hour wasn't enough for the players who had been on the pitch, for them it was like shelling peas, and they just needed a moment or two.

Mata's anguish was understandable, but Mourinho seemed to have found a team that worked, or put better, an eleven which worked. Mata is clearly not a player who is made to be a substitute, especially considering his performances the previous season, but as well as clearly not being a favorite of Mourinho's, unavoidable bad luck and the fact that he found it impossible to be the one player to fix Chelsea's many upheavals also marginalized him.

THE MATCH AT THE ETIHAD STADIUM

At the beginning of February, Chelsea was still in the Premier League title race, and Mourinho had managed to give his team some kind of an identity. But now they came to what looked to be the most difficult game of the season, away to Manchester City, perhaps their biggest title rivals, who had, until then, won all eleven league games played at their stadium.

Chelsea's defense had become one of the most solid in England. In the previous nine games, starting with the 0-0 at Arsenal in December, they had only conceded two goals. Mourinho could feel as confident as at any point in the season and could also thank fate for a game like this arriving precisely at the time when his team was performing best.

But although Chelsea was now picking up all three points fairly regularly, it still hadn't reached that level that Mourinho had talked about some months before. They were winning, but only just, and Mourinho knew that if they went out to play against City as they had done in the previous two months, it might not go well for them. His chicks were fighting to break out of their shells, but they still needed their parent to keep them warm and alive, because winter was still not over.

If he was happy leaving Manchester United in August and Arsenal in December with a goalless draw and he didn't try too hard to win, would it be different now against an opponent that was even more powerful?

Manchester City was winning, entertaining, and scoring goals. They were a better crafted team, with more possession and also in the first season with their manager, Manuel Pellegrini. But Mourinho decided not to go toe to toe, but to resort to a hyper-planned strategy because he simply didn't have a mature enough team.

Mourinho played David Luiz together with Nemanja Matić in defensive midfield to deal with the attacking energy of Manchester City and the organizational power of David Silva; he used Ramires as the third man in the middle of the pitch, gave the inside channels to Hazard and Willian, and put Samuel Eto'o up front. Oscar? He was left on the bench again for a key match.

Manchester City was true to its dominant style, and although Mourinho tried to convince himself that Chelsea was not a team which sat back and hit on the counterattack, that was precisely what it did. City is a team who usually throws a lot of men forward and invites the opposition to attack the spaces it leaves at the back. It's their weak point; every team has one. That day, if we're looking for an excuse, Mourinho had no choice but to do this.

The game took an unexpected turn after thirty-two minutes when Branislav Ivanović reached the edge of the area, shot left-footed, and put Chelsea ahead. Up until then, Mourinho's men had bitten back on occasions and hadn't limited themselves to just parking the bus. In the rest of the game they had some other clear opportunities, but they were unable to take them, while City didn't finish theirs off either and that Monday night ended with one of the most significant twists in the season.

Mourinho takes pride and great satisfaction in winning games like this, although to do so he may have to use an approach that isn't very natural and doesn't offer guarantees of winning. He decided that this was the only way of being able to get something from their visit to the Etihad Stadium on a day as late in the season as February, and this became tangible evidence that Mourinho publicly acknowledged Chelsea's inferiority complex.

If Manchester City had scored just one goal in the first fifteen or twenty minutes we would be talking about a completely different story and that was something that Mourinho couldn't control. Would he have had a master plan to face a situation like that? The difference between how things happened and how they might have happened was almost imperceptible.

One of the things Mourinho had repeated again and again after his arrival the previous summer was that he wanted to build a long-term project and not one for a one-off season. Leaving Oscar on the bench and playing David Luiz in midfield wasn't something he was going to do every day. So why didn't he see that a plan like this for a particular game, whatever the result, wasn't the best way to lead his team along the path he wanted it to take?

Although Manchester City lost that game, they didn't stray from their purest essence, and they managed to keep their momentum going, allowing them to win the title in May. However, Mourinho's plan for that game only achieved a specific objective: three points, which represented a quantitative, but not a qualitative, step forward.

The bitterness Mourinho still carried inside after almost two seasons of perennial inner dissatisfaction, existential turmoil reflected on the pitch, and having to face the most unrewarding version of football, had removed the calmness needed to take on his work in a less stressful way.

Faithful to his guiding principles, he wanted his work to have his own visible stamp, even though this may lead to a series of absurd habits which offered no guarantee of success.

Was it not much easier to adopt a more gradual approach with a more solid base that didn't depend on sporadic master plans and could just as easily end in victory or defeat, or force him to leave on the bench the man he'd praised to the skies since he'd arrived, and who had made it possible for his convoluted and often untranslatable ideas to keep his horse so close to the lead in the title race?

Fate ended up reaffirming, with complete fairness, the team which had been the most solid overall, Manchester City. However, at that moment, Chelsea put down a real marker in the league, sowing a lot of doubts in Pellegrini's team and levelling the title race, which was perhaps the closest-run between so many teams in recent years. At that point, four clubs—Manchester City, Chelsea, Arsenal, and Liverpool—had the chance of ending the season as champions.

Mourinho had clung to a tight nucleus of players. Mohamed Salah arrived in January, but he had barely used him, even when Chelsea's schedule was full of matches and lacking in free weeks. It was almost always the same men who played, and in the last few games he hadn't given much playing time to Schürrle and Demba Ba.

A manager has to monitor the playing time he gives all his players so those who aren't regular starters don't fall into endless inactivity. Keeping them all involved and participating in the footballing direction of the team will allow him to be able to get the best out of them at the times when he's forced to use them.

Twenty or twenty-five minutes at the end of a game which the team is winning comfortably, or a game which is relatively easy, may be just the right amount of football in order for them not to become too frustrated and for all those qualities for which they were signed not to be snatched away. They are in the team for a reason; they didn't get there by divine providence. That gives them confidence. Being sidelined takes it away.

One example which clearly illustrates how important it is to keep all players active can be found in the Tottenham Hotspur team of 2016-2017. Eric Dier had been used as a first-choice midfielder in the previous season because of the injuries to Ryan Mason, Nabil Bentaleb, and Mousa Dembélé, but this year there wasn't so much room for him in the starting lineup, either as a midfielder or as a defender. But to face Chelsea in January, a team on a run of thirteen consecutive victories in the Premier League, Mauricio Pochettino decided to play with three central defenders, one of whom was Dier, and he tried out that system the Sunday before in an easy 4-1 win against Watford.

Spurs beat Chelsea 2-0, with several factors conspiring: the formation chosen by Pochettino; Chelsea's defensive mistakes, which allowed Dele Alli to score twice; Diego Costa's poor finishing with chances that he doesn't usually miss; and Eric Dier's almost flawless performance in the role he was given that day. If Dier hadn't been kept relatively active during the time when he wasn't a regular starter, it would have been impossible for him to give such a stellar performance in such an important game. Dier never stopped feeling important, an active and key cog in a team whose performances encouraged and motivated its own players, and which had a very solid, visible, and constantly evolving identity.

In the case of forwards, they shouldn't only be used when there's an attacking emergency, but should also start some games where the manager can afford the luxury of resting his regular starters, particularly if they are attackers who aren't the typical eternal substitutes, who have something to offer, and whose performances show that they can be trusted to deliver. This allows the manager to have them ready for when he needs them to play a more active part because of the possible absence of the regulars. This, for example, was the case of André Schürrle.

Three weeks after that City game, the first leg of the last sixteen Champions League tie against Galatasaray in Turkey showed that Mourinho had changed his approach. It was the third important match where he had left Oscar out of the starting lineup. His number 10 hadn't played well against West Brom (1-1 draw away) or Everton (1-0 win with an injury-time goal), and the team had found it very hard to build play in a satisfactory way. His presence had also not been too influential in the defeat to Manchester City in the FA Cup. Now, against the Turkish side, Mourinho decided to play Schürrle instead. He didn't want a passer now; he wanted a runner.

Chelsea took an early lead after nine minutes through Fernando Torres, but after twenty minutes of the second half Galatasaray drew level and was threatening to win the game. Mourinho started to panic, quickly replaced Schürrle with John Obi Mikel, and Chelsea focused on purely defensive possession, not trying to use it as an attacking weapon, but instead to eat up time and try to pour cold water on the fire which had been lit in the home team. There followed a huge number of sideways passes to lower the temperature of the match.

Willian, just like Oscar, was removed from the regular starting lineup, and Schürrle took a more active role. This confirms that, with March almost upon him, Mourinho hadn't been able to completely organize his thoughts and his formation hadn't provided a really solid team. In spite of the good run between December and January, his foundations weren't convincingly strong, and Chelsea had again started behaving like a coin tossed in the air. Indeed, now the team's approach was showing its most bitter side, the one with all the doubts, completely unsure of itself. Like at Real Madrid, Mourinho couldn't find peace with himself, and he transmitted this in his decisions. These unexpected changes in the starting lineup changed the established positions on the pitch, because, just like Hazard, Schürrle played on the left.

Perhaps worried by the lack of goals his team were scoring, when they travelled to Fulham on March 1, 2014, Mourinho decided to keep Schürrle as a goal-scoring backup for Fernando Torres, with Willian missing out. In the first half, Chelsea was the same dull, ineffective team as in the previous games, while Schürrle, Hazard, and Oscar rotated areas and roles.

But everything changed in the blink of an eye just after the break. Hazard took on a more influential role in finding a way through, he injected more pace in his movement, and this change paid immediate dividends. André Schürrle scored three goals in fifteen minutes, although this wouldn't have been possible without the key contribution of Fernando Torres, who took the defenders away and created space for the German to arrive unmarked from behind. The Fulham defense helped as well; they were high, slow, and sloppy with their marking.

In January, Chelsea had signed Nemanja Matić because for some reason Mourinho didn't trust Mikel as a holding midfielder. But there was a problem: Matić had played in the Champions League for Benfica in the group stage and could only be registered on the Premier League list of players.

The tie against Galatasaray in the last sixteen was decided without too much trouble in the return leg with two first-half goals, but three days later Chelsea had tripped up badly in the league, losing away at Aston Villa, where they finished with nine men after red cards for Willian and Ramires.

At that stage of the season, we were still wondering exactly which direction Mourinho wanted to take Chelsea. Rather than appreciating a quality product, we were left wondering whether it was a product at all. On seeing what Mourinho did in the following weeks in the most important month in the season, April, those doubts multiplied.

For the visit of Arsenal, Mourinho decided to put David Luiz alongside Matić in defensive midfield, to a certain extent contradicting the formations used in the previous months of the season. Until Matić had arrived, he had played practically without a natural holding midfielder, with Lampard and Ramires both taking on that duty. Now that he had Matić, what made him think that he needed two defensive midfielders in front of the back line?

That game against Arsenal is perhaps not the most trustworthy reference point for this formation, as they were already up 2-0 after seven minutes, and after fifteen Kieran Gibbs was sent off in that famous case of mistaken identity by the referee Andre Marriner, who failed to notice that it had actually been Alex Oxlade-Chamberlain who had intentionally diverted the ball with his arm on the goal line.

The following week, at the hostile home of Crystal Palace, Mourinho used David Luiz alongside Nemanja Matić again, but this time with another change to compound things more. Against Arsenal it had been Oscar who had been the third man in midfield, functioning as a link between his two deeper-lying teammates and the three forwards. Now, against Palace, that position was occupied by Frank Lampard.

Mourinho decided to rest Oscar because the following week they had to play Paris Saint-Germain away in the Champions League, but after selling Mata to Manchester United there was no other player in the Chelsea squad with enough creativity to be able to make up for having two purely defensive players in midfield.

Chelsea was unable to find a way to move the ball out of defense gradually and effectively. The contribution of David Luiz in this task was less than zero; Lampard had already lost all his spark; and Matić, perhaps the one who could naturally have managed it the most effectively, wasn't in a position on the field where he could do so coherently. It wasn't only a question of the players Mourinho had on the pitch; it was also where these players were deployed and how Chelsea wanted to play that didn't in any way help to bring the ball out of defense cleanly.

When Chelsea won the ball back and tried to play it out. The players who could possibly receive the ball, instead of moving toward the man with the ball, did the opposite—they moved away! There was then no choice but to play long balls, which created danger on a couple of occasions, but didn't offer a guarantee of chances and wasn't the right way that Mourinho referred to so much.

To make matters worse, the presence of David Luiz, Matić, and Lampard in midfield didn't offer defensive solidity at all. On the contrary, it slowed them down against a fast team which counterattacked quickly and didn't need to attack with many men in order to create danger.

The evidence was so clear that Mourinho had no choice but to take off David Luiz after the break and allow Oscar to come on and completely transform Chelsea. Forty-five minutes lost in the heat of a fight to the death for the Premier League title.

Fate was fair with Mourinho again; Crystal Palace scored through a John Terry own goal, and Chelsea was practically dropped from the battle with Manchester City and Liverpool.

In the final weeks of the season Mourinho sometimes tried with Schürrle as a center forward—like in the first leg of the Champions League quarter-final against Paris Saint-Germain—but the experiment didn't bear too much fruit, although it seemed a perfectly possible option. Chelsea was submerged again in a dark period which exposed just how ill equipped they were in terms of footballing artillery.

Their full backs, almost always Branislav Ivanović and César Azpilicueta, didn't contribute anything to the attack. David Luiz was a hindrance in midfield, so Oscar was stuck in thick treacle, unable to put moves together quickly and effectively.

For example, at Manchester City, David Silva and Samir Nasri had those spectacular levels of distribution because Yaya Touré and Fernandinho organized the attacking transitions from their base in a way that meant the more advanced players could continue to build the play in a more structured way in the next third of the pitch.

Manchester City, to continue with the same example, attacked more than Chelsea, so they had to work a bit harder to defend, although their high pressing and impressive midfield engine room were highly significant weapons in reducing the risk of being exposed at the back. Vincent Kompany himself acknowledged that the fact that his team concentrated so much on attacking was a great challenge for the defenders.

Mourinho knew that he didn't have attacking machinery like that, so he had to be more compact in defense without attacking full backs. We can say with a high degree of certainty that it wasn't that Mourinho didn't want to attack, but that he'd been unable to put together a model that could do so, and this was exacerbated by the lack of a consistent, goal-scoring center forward, something he had the following season in the shape of Diego Costa. In the long run, the attacking approach of Manchester City prevailed over Chelsea's stingy approach.

The same happened with Brendan Rodgers' Liverpool, who finished above Chelsea in the table, but who lost both meetings against the trap laid by Mourinho, the most cunningly devised of all on that afternoon of Steven Gerrard's historic slip. For Liverpool, that defeat was doubly bitter because Chelsea rested its best players for the return leg of the Champions League semi-final against Atlético de Madrid, and Mourinho designed a plan adapted to fit both the players he sent out onto the pitch and the destructive bent with which he approached that game.

The mentality of both City and Liverpool was very different. Their main objective revolved around creating, rather than forcing, errors from their opponents, or waiting for them to make mistakes because of the pressure they were under to win, which was the strategy Mourinho chose against them.

That's why it wasn't strange that Chelsea won both games against Manchester City and against Liverpool that season but dropped points against teams which played, in Mourinho's words, nineteenth-century football, like West Ham, West Brom, or Sunderland, who did to Chelsea what Mourinho did to City and Liverpool.

Chelsea had a period of around two months from the end of November to the end of January where they played good football, where they were effective and apparently solid, but when the problems arrived and the crisis of his center forwards started to escalate, the solution Mourinho chose was to defend more in order to defend better and thus compensate for the weakness of his attack.

He was no longer satisfied with Oscar and Willian, players he had fully promoted and kept as undisputed starters—even ahead of Mata—and that was when he turned, principally, to Schürrle.

Mourinho, before Nemanja Matić arrived, hadn't been a fan of playing with three less-attacking players in midfield, even though he had John Obi Mikel. But in the last games of the season he used Mikel more and ended up playing a kind of central triumvirate on some occasions in tune with his more defensive strategy.

At this time, there was an alarming loss of influence exerted by Oscar, and Chelsea continued to be a side tossed about in the wind, while Mourinho was a little more flexible with his more advanced players. Schürrle played more because he offered a goal-scoring alternative to the dismal form of his forwards, and the fact that they were still in the Champions League meant he had to rotate his players.

Summer brought with it the arrival of Francesc Fàbregas and Diego Costa, which, together with the consolidation of Nemanja Matić in midfield, filled the gaps from the previous season. Chelsea started to look like a more streamlined product, more like the direction Mourinho had suggested months before.

Fàbregas started like a real assist-providing machine, Diego Costa found any net that was put in front of him, while Eden Hazard was the golden piece of the jigsaw, the man who kept the side's confidence levels high and who everyone gave the ball to when things got hard.

Mourinho continued to cling to a new group of players and to play almost every game with the same starting lineup. Courtois, Terry, Cahill, Ivanović, Azpilicueta, Matić, Fàbregas, Willian, Hazard, and Diego Costa were practically fixed starters, and in the difficult away games he repeatedly used Mikel in midfield alongside Matić, moving Fàbregas to the position usually occupied by Oscar.

Ramires, Filipe Luis, Loïc Rémy, and Schürrle played very little and Mohamed Salah never. Didier Drogba got the minutes befitting his age, his fitness, and his role in the squad. He even played more than Rémy.

Not even in the League Cup semi-final, a competition often used to give playing time to those who don't get much otherwise, did Mourinho depart from his trusted players. That's why when he did try to give them a chance for an apparently easy game against Bradford City in the FA Cup, Chelsea fell apart in the second half, conceded four goals, and said goodbye to the tournament, despite having been 2-0 up.

Mourinho was more obsessed by the big prizes—the Premier League and the Champions League—and the team had enough in the tank to launch a strong bid for both competitions. Chelsea became the most complete side in the Premier League and acquired a well-established and functional style to win games.

In the second half of the 2014-2015 season, although they didn't start dropping points alarmingly, Chelsea's play was less effective. Undeniable proof of this was the decreasing influence of Fàbregas in creating opportunities, the drop in his number of assists, and Diego Costa's injury woes.

All of this showed Mourinho's most insecure side again, the one which, when he takes a very hard-fought lead, means he has to protect it by all means available, instead of remaining true to the role Chelsea had then: the outright leader and Premier League champions elect.

Being knocked out of the Champions League in the last sixteen by Paris Saint-Germain was a bitter blow, but Mourinho's lineup for the return leg, with Matić, Ramires, Fàbregas, and Oscar in midfield, and the limp manner in which the team performed on the pitch with an extra man for an hour and a half, show the fears Mourinho has in taking on a more active role in those situations where he has to grab the bull by the horns. It's as if he couldn't let go of his fear and his inferiority complex against the big teams, and only a lobotomy could give him back the audacity he once had, but which in his spell at Real Madrid seems to have been ripped from him.

Against PSG, Mourinho felt unsure of what his players could achieve if he played with a balanced, but attacking, formation, just like the one he used in 95 percent of situations. There are moments where you must crush your opponent when they stumble, and you can't allow them to get back up again. Mourinho finds it hard to do this because he no longer has it in his DNA.

Worrying about how to cancel out your opponent is key, vital, but you can't allow the stubbornness in achieving it to end up inhibiting the strengths of your own players. Stimulating a mentality like this takes ambition away from players, and that wonderful abandon which playing football produces, whether based on controlling the ball or the space, is locked away from them.

MOURINHO'S FIRST YEAR AT MANCHESTER UNITED—REDISCOVERY

Mourinho must have endured the longest and most trying days of his life between being sacked by Chelsea and finding out that he was going to be the next Manchester United manager. The dissatisfaction he felt at the disaster which occurred at Stamford Bridge between August and December 2015 made him desperately want to return to the bench to prove to himself and the world that this had just been one very, very small gray page on his CV, something which could and had to be put right immediately.

Mourinho had the necessary financial resources to strengthen the team just as he wanted. Eric Bailly in the center of the defense, Paul Pogba in midfield, Henrikh Mkhitaryan as playmaker, and Zlatan Ibrahimović spearheading the attack.

At the start of the season Mourinho was too naive to realize that Pogba and Fellaini were not cut out to play on their own in midfield. This is firstly because neither of them is a real holding midfielder and secondly because if you put them that far back two things happen: either they focus on their defensive work and the team is deprived of their attacking power, or they aren't going to carry out their defensive duties properly because their instinct will lead them to think more about attacking, and they'll leave spaces in front of the defense. That was exactly what happened in the defeat at Old Trafford against Guardiola's Manchester City on September 10.

As is customary with him, that day Mourinho complained about penalties not being given, but he never mentioned the fact that even if those penalties had been awarded, it wouldn't have changed the fact that his team had played badly. He didn't hold back from openly criticizing his players either. "*I didn't want to make three changes at half-time, but if it was a sport with a free number of changes … I would have done it after twenty minutes,*" he said.

After losing against City, Manchester United gave another tepid performance in the defeat against Feyenoord in the Europa League. Although this time Mourinho did decide to play three midfielders —Schneiderlin, Pogba, and Ander Herrera—United looked like van Gaal's team: disjointed, dull, with no really effective idea of how to move the ball and attack.

Three days later, away at Watford, Mourinho decided to use Pogba and Fellaini alone in the midfield again and had an attacking rush of blood to the head which led to him playing Wayne Rooney, Marcus Rashford, Anthony Martial, and Zlatan Ibrahimović as forwards. Rooney played a little farther back, as if he were trying to compensate for playing the three forwards and the manifest fragility of that midfield.

But Rooney, Pogba, and company kept misplacing easy passes, there still was no collective dynamic to bring out the best of each of these players, and Mourinho hadn't yet discovered what system would best suit the players he had in the squad. Pogba was under too much pressure to play like the most expensive player in history and that affected his level of performance. Manchester United lost their third game in a row.

Mourinho was still determined to use two players in midfield without either of them being a natural holding midfielder. The only player in the team with those characteristics was Michael Carrick, whom he considered too old (35) to be used consistently and made into one of the key members of the team.

At Anfield, one month after the defeat against Watford, Mourinho still didn't play Carrick, preferring Ander Herrera as a support for Pogba and Fellaini in midfield, but Manchester United continued to limp along at half power. Mourinho tried everything, except Michael Carrick. Perhaps he didn't see or nobody told him about the change United experienced in the previous season when Carrick returned from his injury. His form was so decisive that he earned a contract extension of one more season.

That day against Liverpool, October 17, Manchester United restricted themselves to defending deep, having 35 percent possession, and one shot on target and one corner.

Liverpool had two clear chances, one for Emre Can and the other for Philippe Coutinho, both saved by David de Gea. The match finished goalless, but José Mourinho said that Manchester United controlled the game tactically and emotionally and that the two chances Liverpool created were "*out of context*." If we analyze his words carefully, we can see that his intention was purely to defend, not to lose, which is why he thinks that they controlled everything, and he was happy. If attacking and having a greater chance of winning had also been important to him, then he would have realized that his team didn't play well because they barely created any chances.

Mourinho claimed that the Liverpool chances were "*out of context*" because they were unable to translate all their possession into a siege on the Manchester United goal. Liverpool tried to get through, came up against an opponent who sat back, and they had no choice but to move the ball around to try and find a pass or a cross to unlock the door to score. It wasn't a constant siege, but neither were the chances "*out of context*" because Liverpool had the ball more in the final third, attacked more, and United defended very close to their own area. If Mourinho had been interested in attacking, then there's no way that he could say that they controlled the game.

If Liverpool had scored from one of the two clear chances they had, would the goal not have counted because it was "*out of context?*"

One week later, at Stamford Bridge, Mourinho hadn't finished parking the bus when Chelsea went ahead in the first minute. United ended up conceding four, and Mourinho suffered one of the biggest humiliations of his career. This, clearly, wasn't a defeat out of context.

This disaster practically wiped out all the progress (?) which might have been made since the start of the season, and Mourinho tried to get out of the slump by giving more playing time to the players who were in better form. For example, when Mkhitaryan returned from injury in November and started creating a lot of chances, he became a fixture in the starting lineup. He clung on to the players who were playing best.

Mourinho encountered Juan Mata again at Manchester United, who had fled from Chelsea precisely because he'd been marginalized by Mourinho. The use or not of Mata was one of the questions that created the most expectation after Mourinho arrived at Old Trafford. But unlike what happened at Chelsea, Mourinho did consistently use Mata, who now had no Oscar to provide competition for the number 10 position.

After the victory against Watford on February 11, Mourinho said:

> *When I came here people thought Mata was in trouble but I knew he wouldn't be in trouble. One thing was the football I wanted my Chelsea to play and the other thing I want my Manchester United to play. Mata has adapted to the football I want to play. I knew since the beginning he would be an important player. I think he feels that confidence in me. He is happy on the pitch and you can see it the way he plays.*

Now that he had a group of different players, perhaps Mourinho did design a slightly different plan at Manchester United, albeit with basically the same principles. But it's not as though he suddenly changed to playing with Barça or Bayern Munich levels of possession overnight or had a team that just lived for counterattacking like the Leicester City team that won the league the season before. We can infer, then, that the real change was in how Mata functioned: at Chelsea in one way and at Manchester United in another.

That day against Watford, United were let loose, playing with four natural forwards: Mata, Anthony Martial, Mkhitaryan, and Zlatan. They only won 2-0, but they created countless opportunities and played a style of football that fans always like to see at Old Trafford. This was the starting lineup that Mourinho chose for that game, foreseeing the dominance his team might enjoy and the weak opposition Watford would offer, but it wasn't a lineup that had been tried and tested over time.

So if Mourinho used it again and allowed himself to be carried away with what had happened on that particular day—more or less as he had before with Mkhitaryan—it would be an acknowledgment that the idea of football he wanted to implant at Manchester United hadn't developed very far. A team has to be able to play well with three or four forwards, with two or three midfielders, as long as there is a balance between its players and a coherent and applicable concept of play.

Using Pogba in a two-man midfield would also have meant involving him in too many defensive duties again. Mourinho could see the reflection of the Brendan Rodgers' Liverpool team looking back at him in the mirror; Rodgers seized the moment, almost won the Premier League in 2014, and from the following season onward never found the same fluency again. Getting carried away by the moment doesn't mean long-term solidity. The team must be tactically flexible and comfortable with all variations. Against a strong opponent that is a real threat going forward, Manchester United weren't going to unleash the offensive firepower that they showed against Watford when playing with those four forwards or set up entirely defensively either.

Little by little, Mourinho started to realize the need to use Michael Carrick more in order to allow the other midfielders and the attackers to be able to carry out their duties better. Even at the age of thirty-five, there was no other player in the United squad with his defensive instincts in midfield, his calmness in moving the ball under pressure, or his precision in passing the ball forward. In the League Cup final against Southampton, Mourinho left him out of the starting eleven, and at the start of the second half he was forced to bring him on because Pogba and Ander Herrera couldn't cope on their own. Once Carrick had settled, United took control of the game and ended up winning it with a Zlatan goal near the end.

Putting a man like Carrick in the defensive area of the midfield not only provided perfect balance to the team, but it also allowed Pogba to revel in the same conditions he'd enjoyed at Juventus, which led to his transfer fee being the highest in history.

The price of a player doesn't decide his context. Pogba performed at "a value of £89 million" at Juventus, but that doesn't mean that he will do so at Manchester United if he's given other roles. It didn't make much sense to pay that amount of money and then use him in a different context. But it took Mourinho a few months to realize this.

Indeed, Mourinho might have missed a trick in the summer by not creating those conditions. If he didn't plan to use Carrick too much, then he could have foregone the signing of Bailly or Mkhitaryan, for example, positions where he already had enough players, to bring in someone who could consistently play next to Pogba and who would allow him to release all his potential.

To form a solid team and shake off the pessimism engendered during the Louis van Gaal era, it wasn't a bad idea at all to play with three in midfield, thus making the team firm and impassable, allowing that solid midfield to become the best ally of both the defense and the attack.

He took his time, but Mourinho did finally realize this, and Carrick found a lot more opportunities in the first team, although he was forced to rotate given the situation of having to play twice a week all season. Ander Herrera also became a key player in the midfield because of his ability to participate so well in both types of transition, and Manchester United at least acquired a defensive solidity, allowing them to remain unbeaten in the Premier League from the embarrassing defeat at Stamford Bridge in October until the game against Arsenal on May 7.

However, despite that ability to contain their opponents, there was still no clear visible identity, no finely tuned end product, as there had been with Mourinho's Chelsea team which won the 2014-2015 Premier

League title. A place in the top four escaped Manchester United because of the constant insipid home draws, those games where the team was supposed to be freer and play their best football, but where they often felt more repressed and devoid of ideas.

In the Europa League, United knocked out Rostov, Anderlecht, and Celta de Vigo by the tightest of margins, and there was the feeling that if they'd played a more substantial opponent, they might not have gotten to the final. Indeed, they won the final against Ajax having less of the ball and fewer shots on goal, and with two goals we could certainly describe as *out of context*.

It is true that it was Mourinho's first season, he suffered a blight of injuries, and they played two games a week right up until the cup final, but beyond the results, the feeling remained that with their squad, Manchester United could have been a little more pleasing on the eye.

Could it be that the dissatisfaction Mourinho experienced during his stay at Real Madrid and at Chelsea was still affecting the way he managed and cast a shadow over his ability to construct a successful team? Could it be that his players lacked that feeling of freedom and fulfilment they need to play at their best?

The next season(s) for Manchester United will offer a clear verdict on the transformation undergone by the manager who was the most sought after in the world a decade ago.

Chapter 8

LOUIS VAN GAAL AND BRENDAN RODGERS—THE FRUITLESS SEARCH

One of the consequences of post-modern football and the amount of money moving around in it is the lack of patience many of the big clubs have with their managers. One season without trophies can be enough to get the sack, even if we're talking about a manager with a solid résumé who won important trophies in the previous season with the same club.

Calmness is in ever shorter supply, so the pressure managers work under is alarmingly huge. The Bundesliga is a rare case; there, the trend hasn't fully caught on, and tolerance is still the norm, but in a not insignificant number of big European clubs, the policy of "now or never" is practiced.

English football in particular, one of the most competitive leagues in the world, has been taken over by several rich owners who see the management of their clubs purely as a business. The sporting aspect is just a vehicle to make more money—although many haven't managed to—and in some cases the means employed defy belief.

However, in many others, and because of that pressure that all managers are familiar with, mistakes in managing teams sometimes leave us helpless to defend those who have been removed from their posts. Of course, there's also the exception to this, which is Arsène Wenger.

The most recent story in this game of thrones and power, which was played out concisely and mysteriously but had an ending as merciless as other, more predictable ones, was the sacking of Louis van Gaal by Manchester United. It was an atypical and even treacherous split, because Ed Woodward, the executive vice chairman of the club, waited until the day following the FA Cup had been won to tell him that he'd no longer be in charge of the squad, while at the same time plotting behind his back to replace him with José Mourinho.

Before the game against Bournemouth, his last in the Premier League and the penultimate game of the season, van Gaal had again shown his annoyance with the press for their continual speculation about his future. "*I am very angry and I have shown that many, many times. But in spite of the attacks of the media – and not only the media, the legends* [Paul Scholes] *and other kinds of people – I am here and I am fighting … I am an open book for everybody*," he said.[41]

At that point, he still believed that he would complete the three seasons he had signed for after the 2014 World Cup, and he didn't imagine that that would be his last week at Old Trafford.

"*I believe in myself*," he added. "*I believe in Manchester United. I believe in the players. I hope that everybody is believing like me, then it is much more easier*," he finished.

Louis van Gaal believed right up to the last moment that his bosses trusted him and that the inconsistency of the team—one day able to brush Liverpool aside, another getting thrashed by MK Dons—would not be given more importance than his experience, his trophy cabinet, and the opportunities he had given to the youth academy players. Although a very conservative approach by Ed Woodward might have allowed him to see out the last year of his contract, there weren't many arguments left to save him from the guillotine falling to hasten his early departure.

Louis van Gaal's first season, 2014-2015, was like a football pitch. We can divide it in thirds according to the different tactical formations he employed. He suddenly changed from playing three at the back to a back four, only to go back to his initial choice. Ander Herrera and Juan Mata were regular starters at times, while at others they barely got on the pitch.

In his first games in charge, Louis van Gaal decided to try a three-man defense with Antonio Valencia and Ashley Young playing as wing backs, both good wingers, but not reliable defenders when this is required as an important part of their duties. It isn't that playing with three at the back is counterproductive, but Manchester United were simply not prepared enough to play like that.

This was shown in the fourth league game of the season, just after coming back from the September international break. United played at home against Queens Park Rangers, van Gaal played with a back four, with Rafael and Marcos Rojo as full backs, and won comfortably 4-0, the biggest victory of the whole season and one of the best performances by the team under his management.

The defensive work was so tremendous that Daley Blind was able to play as a holding midfielder without being a natural there, while Ander Herrera concentrated exclusively on passing the ball around in the opposition's half. However, there was a feeling that van Gaal was allowing a style of play that was too open, end to end, when what the team really needed was to regain the confidence it had lost after Sir Alex Ferguson's departure, and that could only be achieved by adopting a more dominant style.

One month later, playing away to West Brom, Manchester United had to come from behind twice to rescue a draw. van Gaal again played Blind and Herrera in midfield, and after the break, down 1-0, he replaced Herrera with Marouane Fellaini.

Fellaini had the same freedom the Spaniard had had in the first half, and a few minutes after coming on he scored a great equalizer. van Gaal was clear that he wasn't interested in the two men who were nominally playing in front of the back four staying close to them when the team were mounting an attacking transition or were attacking, when just one was enough.

On that day, Manchester United showed their wobbly side and needed a last-gasp equalizer to escape with a point. While van Gaal could allow himself a more attacking formation against a team like West Brom, who were not so solid, he needed to use the easier games to create certain patterns that would give the team solidity when they played against stronger opposition. This was still a team under construction, rediscovering itself, which most of all needed to have self-confidence and be strong in defense to then gradually extend that strength to the other areas of the team.

Against Chelsea the following week, he started with Fellaini, and when Manchester United gained possession of the ball, the Belgian would move quickly to the penalty area to wait for a cross, but he didn't participate much in the very vertical creation of play. That was left solely to Ángel Di María, Juan Mata, and Adnan Januzaj.

He offset having Fellaini in the opposition's area all the time with his full backs not going forward very much; in other words, he basically had five men at the back—the four defenders and Daley Blind. In the first half no balls came to Fellaini in the air, and it was going to be difficult for him to win them if they did, as he was battling with John Terry, Gary Cahill, and Branislav Ivanović. It wasn't a case of him always being beaten in the air though—no, the ball just never came to him.

On many occasions, when Chelsea won the ball back in midfield, Fellaini had to hurry back to help his team out in defense. He was late to cover, he didn't support his full backs, and he allowed Chelsea superiority on some occasions. Fortunately for United, Chelsea didn't respond with dazzling counterattacks, instead making more gradual, and therefore less direct, attacking transitions. For that simple reason, they didn't suffer too much.

So would it not have been better to put Fellaini in midfield and help the team bring the ball out more safely through tidier possession, which would allow Di María and Januzaj to get into more dangerous positions? Let's put it like this: Those two players help out a lot in defense, but their defensive duties increase if one of the two deeper-lying midfielders is always in the opposition's penalty area, as was the case with Fellaini.

This style of play by van Gaal, putting Fellaini up as a "false 9" to look for the ball in between the opposition center backs, wasn't the way to give United the solidity they needed to gradually acquire. It's not the case that there is just one way to make a team solid, but it does make sense to go for the way that is most likely to succeed. Besides, that wasn't a sensible way to attack either.

In the next game, Manchester United lost 1-0 against Manchester City, having been left with ten men in the thirty-ninth minute because of Chris

Smalling's sending off. In the second half, the team didn't crumble, and they put up a reasonable show, although van Gaal himself acknowledged that the ball was lost in dangerous areas, and they didn't keep possession in situations where they should have done.

But can you really expect to play Januzaj, Di María, Rooney, and Van Persie and have quality possession? These were the gaps in coherence under van Gaal. He left Mata on the bench and put out a lineup that invited immediate verticality, but he wanted possession.

After that defeat, Manchester United put together six consecutive Premier League victories, the last a comfortable 3-0 win over Liverpool at Old Trafford. Michael Carrick started to play phenomenally well as a holding midfielder and in moving the ball forward toward the more advanced players. He became United's best performing player. Fellaini floated in front of him when the team had the ball and moved back to the base of the midfield when they lost it.

If a team plays with three center backs and two wing backs, it's understandable in a way that they should only need one holding midfielder. But if they use a conventional defensive line it becomes more of a risk to play with only one defensive midfielder and five clearly defined attackers, which is what van Gaal did at home against Leicester City and away against West Ham United.

In the West Ham game, those five forwards—Di María, Januzaj, Rooney, Van Persie, and Falcao—barely created any clear-cut chances because the team wasn't set up in a structured way. It was a good example that no matter how many forwards you throw onto the pitch, you don't get profoundly attacking machinery if behind them the team isn't ticking over sensibly. Manchester United had returned to the path of shadows and arrogance, and van Gaal showed that after six months of the season he still didn't have his ideas straight in his head. In February, there was nothing left of that impressive run that had finished in December against Liverpool. Those weeks marked the first indications of Wayne Rooney moving to a deeper-lying position on the pitch, something that later became a reality.

Then, at Newcastle, after repeatedly playing him in midfield, van Gaal started a string of five games where he returned Rooney to the center forward position and used fewer forwards and more midfielders in his starting lineup. Now Ander Herrera was used in midfield alongside Michael Carrick, while Fellaini functioned as a sort of second forward, something the Dutch manager hadn't tried all season before that. They won those five games, and the last of them, coincidentally, was another comfortable win against Liverpool in the game where Steven Gerrard was sent off for sinking his studs into Ander Herrera when he hadn't been on the pitch for a minute.

Up to that point, if there was one thing which hadn't been missing from van Gaal's reign, it was experiments and multiple tactical approaches. Rooney had played almost as a holding midfielder, as a second forward, and as a lone striker, like at Anfield. Fellaini had been played deeper and higher up on the pitch, had performed man-marking duties, and had waited for crosses in the area like another forward. Now he was given the freedom to play in front of two holding midfielders without having to perform so many defensive duties.

Weeks before, when van Gaal had used him in approximately that same position, but with two center forwards in front of him, Fellaini barely participated in the attacking transitions because those two men were the reference point for the attack and because the area linking the top of the second third of the pitch with the start of the third was purely a transit area, rather than a creative one, and the ball was usually moved out to the wings.

It could be said that Fellaini is a special player because to get the best out of what he should offer, he needs to play in a particular position. He's not a man you can let loose on the pitch and expect to open things up wherever he goes. David Moyes—the man who took him to Old Trafford on the last day of the 2013 transfer window—tried him alongside Michael Carrick in defensive midfield to start with, but he soon realized that it didn't make much sense not to use him in more attacking areas, as he had done at Everton.

Fellaini requires a certain amount of space to feel comfortable and to be able to link with the rest of the team. When he arrived, he was a player with characteristics that were somewhat different to what Manchester United was used to, as was Shinji Kagawa. Ultimately, he's not a holding midfielder, or a forward, or a playmaker, and certainly not a winger, but he is a player who is able to fill in excellently in all these positions on given occasions within a game. van Gaal now seemed to have found a very wise way to get the best out of him: by allowing him to win the ball in his own area one moment and bring it down on his chest on the edge of the opposition's area another moment, or get his head on the end of a cross from the wing. The key lay in having the freedom of a second forward and the mind of a midfielder.

Juan Mata, having been relegated to the bench in the second of the three thirds of United's campaign, became a regular starter again as a result of Ángel Di María's red card in the FA Cup game against Arsenal in March and was a fixture in the starting eleven until the end of the season. The Argentine never started a game again that season.

Almost all the players in the Manchester United squad had enough quality to be important parts of a winning team, but after so many months and so many variations, there was a feeling that van Gaal couldn't decide on a formation and on specific positions that would best exploit the talent of the squad.

Having dominant players in the middle of the field who make the team a little more impenetrable and keep the ball better is a good way to put a lost team back on track. But above all else, a manager must keep in mind at all times the fact that his players perform better when they play in a specific position, in a specific system, and with specific teammates. To achieve this, continuity is needed, rather than so many tactical changes that the players and the manager himself end up confused.

The judgment passed on van Gaal which condemned him for taking so long to find a stable, functional, solid, and attractive formation, was not too unfair. Despite having achieved the minimum objective of qualifying for the Champions League—or rather, its qualifying round—the team's lack of self-confidence was like a cancer eating away at it from the inside. Of the last six 2014-2015 Premier League games, Manchester United only won one.

In his second season, van Gaal didn't offer much cause to be protected from the constant criticism that rained down on him. Several new players arrived, those he didn't want left, but Manchester United continued to look like a product trying to find a way to be built, but was unable to do so.

In the previous season he agreed to bring Radamel Falcao on loan and add him to the three center forwards who were already in the squad at the time—Wayne Rooney, Robin van Persie, and Danny Welbeck—although the latter would end up being transferred to Arsenal as the transfer window closed. Once Falcao's loan spell had ended, Van Persie had left for Fenerbahçe and Chicharito had been sold to Bayer Leverkusen when he came back from Real Madrid's loan, he was left with Wayne Rooney as his only center forward. Anthony Martial arrived just before the transfer window closed in a deal that was pushed through in great panic and haste.

Van Persie had been van Gaal's standard-bearer at the top of the attack for Holland in the Brazil World Cup. In their first season together at Manchester United, injuries meant that he didn't play regularly, and, as the player himself confirmed in an interview with *The Sunday Times*, he even asked to play in the reserve team to recover his form, but van Gaal never believed in him again.

Van Persie said, after arriving in Turkey:

> *The atmosphere changed between me and Louis and people at the club saw it, but I was always professional. I was still thinking we could come back from holiday and start from scratch, but when I came back it wasn't an honest battle any more. Fighting to get back in the team wasn't given to me as an option.*[42]

Instead of being the Theatre of Dreams, Old Trafford became the Colosseum of Yawns. The team's possession of the ball, the highest in the league, was completely sterile, dull, and horizontal—too many meaningless touches that didn't unbalance the opposition or find a way through to goal. van Gaal's second and last season saw Manchester United record their lowest number of goals since the old Division One in 1990, with just forty-nine.

The low point came with the defeat by Norwich on December 19 at Old Trafford, which ended up empty so that fans didn't have to watch that bloody ending. You couldn't believe your eyes—and the memory of it is still less credible.

van Gaal never felt close to his players. He always had his pad in his hands, sitting on the bench, taking everything down, a long way from the action. He never approached the pitch to give instructions, or just so his players didn't feel alone. You don't have to be a Cholo Simeone, a Guardiola, or a Mourinho here, but when you're managing men in such a dynamic environment as football, proximity inspires confidence and liberates players.

One of the few occasions when he left his seat was that unforgettable moment against Arsenal when he slipped in front of Mike Dean to complain about a clear dive.

van Gaal didn't realize how useful Ángel Di María could be for him and that being a player's friend was the best way to enhance his performance on the pitch, as well as the relationship between them. He was never able to get the best out of Anthony Martial, and he confined him too much to the left wing. A team which finds it so difficult to score goals should have their best finishers closest to the goal. With Mata, something similar happened; he played him wide on the right and didn't allow him to be the one responsible for transforming Manchester United's style of play. Mata could easily have been the catalyst for more effective possession, but it's impossible to be able to encourage your teammates to be less predictable and more inventive with the ball when you feel so isolated and are so close to the touchline.

To a certain extent van Gaal ended up facing the consequences of something he wasn't completely responsible for, but ended up having an enormous effect on his stay at Old Trafford. Indeed, the first weeks when José Mourinho was in charge confirm the size of that phenomenon.

Speaking to the *Manchester Evening News*, David Gill, the former chief executive of Manchester United, said this: "*The very fact that Manchester United were winning trophies on a regular basis under* [Sir] *Alex* [Ferguson], *people wanted to come and play for him.*"[43]

The first person to pay the price for the departure not only of Ferguson, but also of Gill in the same year (2013), was David Moyes. van Gaal inherited a club image which was no longer such a draw when it came to attracting world-class players like Ruud van Nistelrooy, Nemanja Vidić, or Patrice Evra. This, together with his lack of know-how for managing the club, was a recipe for the poisonous cocktail which prized him from the post before the end of his contract.

And it's not that van Gaal doesn't measure up to Alex Ferguson, if you want to make that rather odious comparison, but the sum of Ferguson plus his Manchester United is lightyears ahead of the same equation if we substitute the name of the Scottish genius for that of the Dutch manager. The club's pulling power for footballers was no longer the same.

Mourinho—without being better or worse as a manager than van Gaal or Ferguson—is at least a more charismatic, more possessive figure who doesn't rest until he's achieved what he wants to. Bringing Paul Pogba back is something van Gaal would never have thought of, but all the Portuguese had to do was wish for it to happen, and it did. So, while Manchester United may be "buying" their way back to success and their academy may not play such an important part in providing young players for the first team, the figure of Ferguson as a magnet for footballers isn't missed so much now.

van Gaal didn't survive the media firing squad and their constant stories and questions either. Quite apart from the team's dismal form, the media harassment directly and indirectly affected his work, which made him more furious and less rational. These days it's more difficult for a manager to maintain professional stability—especially in the big English clubs, with the exception of Arsenal—when they know that the margin for error is minimal. Now everything is played out in the public domain, it's impossible to hide something, and if Mourinho's out of work and crying out for a swift return to management in the Premier League, can a greater pressure be found? The press didn't give van Gaal a single week's respite and he didn't do much to put a stop to the hullabaloo following him around. This is twenty-first century football, ruthless as never before, a wild west showdown where life is preserved at gunpoint.

Ultimately, nothing happened to van Gaal that hasn't happened before to any other manager; he hit a bad spell. Indeed, this wasn't something which had happened frequently in his career, because apart from his time at Old Trafford, his second spell at Barça and Holland missing out on qualification for the 2002 World Cup, in the rest of his jobs he had achieved stellar success. His failure at United was down to a mixture of inflexibility, whims, inability, and a little bad luck.

One of the results of Louis van Gaal's time at Manchester United which now seems irreversible is Wayne Rooney's move back from his center forward position. One of the Dutchman's craziest ideas was to move him back to midfield, although when all the other forwards left he had no choice but to move him back to spearhead the attack.

There's no doubt that Rooney had lost a lot of his goal-scoring threat and that Manchester United could no longer trust him as their lone striker. Rooney has also shown that he's effective as a second forward and has an almost unique ability to sacrifice himself to help his teammates in the most uncomfortable defensive duties, even when he's playing as a center forward. This, without a doubt, made him an even better player.

Rooney is capable of going from the opposition's penalty area to his own area to recover the ball, or of clearing a ball off the line. When in a particular game the team urgently needed a committed midfielder, all eyes inevitably turned to Wayne Rooney.

But little by little all these ingredients became mixed together. Rooney started playing deeper and deeper, didn't do at all badly by the standards of that Manchester United side, and the approach continued. It was the result of an unexpected chain of events which included the team's upheavals and the uncertain stewardship of van Gaal.

Being very good beyond his primary function ended up transforming Rooney in the final stage of his career and accelerated his decline, because he won't be the forward he once was again and won't be a top midfielder either. Now he depends on his team's play not to look like a complete disaster and has fallen into that positional limbo in which he also found himself with England during the European Championship in 2016 and where he seemed to have no utility to Manchester United in any function. Now back at Everton, he needs to rediscover himself as a player.

BRENDAN RODGERS—SOLIDITY IS NOT BORN FROM A TACTICAL CHANGE OVERNIGHT, HOWEVER MUCH THIS MAY SEEM TO BE THE CASE

Louis van Gaal's first season at Manchester United shared certain similarities with Brendan Rodgers' time at Liverpool. His was a spell which also left notable heartache, even though he was on the point of winning an inconceivable Premier League title, something which Manchester United have not been within sniffing distance of since Sir Alex Ferguson left.

After a first season that was perhaps below expectations but within acceptable boundaries, Liverpool was just one small slip away from becoming the king of football in England again twenty-four years on. However, that magical recovery faded away the following season after the sale of Luis Suárez, Sturridge's injuries, and the arrival of several new players to the squad.

In a period of three days between December 26 and 29, 2013, in Brendan Rodgers' second season at Anfield, Liverpool played their two most difficult games of that Premier League season. An evil trick of the fixture schedule. They had just won four games in a row very comfortably, scoring seventeen goals including ten from Luis Suárez, but they lost 2-1 twice, at Manchester City and at Chelsea. In both cases they went ahead in the game but were behind by half-time. They dropped from top spot at Christmas to fifth place by the new year.

Despite all the similarities, these were two very different games that Rodgers will never forget. Against City, they went toe to toe, but against Chelsea they were unable to whip up anything like the maelstrom that had had the sky-blue team against the ropes. Thursday teemed with goal-scoring opportunities, but on Sunday they were noticeable by their absence.

The key to such a difference in just seventy-two hours was the performance of their midfield. Pellegrini's City was a team that liked to play and allowed the opposition to play, which is why Liverpool found so much space in the City penalty area. But Mourinho's Chelsea neither played nor allowed the opposition to, and the budding functionality of the team that Rodgers was intent on setting up was tied up in knots by their web.

On both occasions the Northern Irish manager used three midfielders and three attackers, the same formation that had achieved the four comfortable wins mentioned above. What Liverpool was missing was the flexibility to allow that formation to work the same against mid-table sides as against their biggest title rivals.

Less than a month later, on January 18 against Aston Villa, Rodgers made a surprising and rather counterproductive change. He played Steven Gerrard and Jordan Henderson alone in midfield, and ahead of them four forwards, Raheem Sterling, Coutinho, Daniel Sturridge, and Luis Suárez.

In principle, Aston Villa—at that time a team in much better form than the one which went down recently—weren't the kind of simple opponent that you could experiment like this against. Especially because they played with three very dangerous forwards in Andreas Weimann, Gabriel Agbonlahor, and Christian Benteke, which required an opposition midfield to isolate them and force at least two of them to come deeper, as Arsenal had done the week before.

Indeed, there were still a lot of doubts about whether Gerrard and Henderson were cut out for playing alone in midfield with four very attack-minded players ahead of them. It was a sudden and surprising change because the team hadn't been playing badly with Lucas Leiva or Joe Allen forming quite a functional sort of central triumvirate.

When Aston Villa won the ball back they were able to keep it for considerably long periods because Liverpool wasn't reactive in recovering it and didn't have a formation on the pitch which allowed an effective press after losing it. The villains went ahead 2-0, and just before half-time Daniel Sturridge got one back.

Although they were behind and on paper the change might be seen as a defensive one, in practice it wasn't. Brendan Rodgers took Coutinho off and put Lucas Leiva on at the start of the second half because the advantage Liverpool was giving up in the midfield was clear.

The momentum shifted entirely the other way, and Aston Villa didn't function nearly as well in the second half, particularly because Liverpool tightened up a lot in midfield and found it easier to break down their opponents' play. They no longer had to defend as close to their own area, and so their own build-ups started much farther forward. Lucas was injured twenty minutes after coming on, but Joe Allen, his replacement, was able to continue the same sort of dynamic established by the Brazilian.

The equalizer came eight minutes into the second half when Suárez tricked the referee to win a penalty, but although they had over half an hour left, Liverpool was unable to find a winner. They had dropped two points at home against easier opposition, which left them lagging behind in the title race. But Brendan Rodgers had an idea he wanted to try, and he wasn't going to give up on it so easily.

After thrashing Everton 4-0 the following week at Anfield with four natural forwards—to a certain extent forced because Lucas and Allen were injured—they then had to travel to West Brom. Rodgers again used Gerrard, Henderson, and the same four forwards, and that day Liverpool played better than they had against Aston Villa, but worse than against Everton, and closer to badly than to well.

They went ahead in the first half, but the Baggies equalized halfway through the second half after a mistake by Kolo Touré, and darkness fell on them. Rodgers was forced to bring on Allen for Coutinho again to stabilize the midfield, although that brought the loss of a little dynamism in attack as a result, but the team was crying out for that balance, and he had no choice. Indeed, they didn't suffer much more because West Brom put up a fight in midfield but not in the Liverpool penalty area, because their attackers weren't very convincing; this was very different to what had happened against Aston Villa.

Rodgers realized then that he couldn't use the same formation against all opponents or in all situations, and that he'd have to play according to the context. He would make up for having two men in midfield by bringing the four forward players back almost into their own half when the team lost the ball, and as a result this allowed him to make the most of their speed when bringing the ball out. When the opponents didn't cover the spaces well when they lost the ball in dangerous areas, playing with just two men in front of the defense worked well for him, but when they didn't allow the smallest concessions, like West Brom, the system became cumbersome.

With Gerrard, Henderson, Coutinho, Sterling, Sturridge, and Suárez, Liverpool jumped on Arsenal like a wild beast and scored four goals in twenty minutes. They then managed two hard-fought wins against Fulham and Swansea, where they very much reacted to the situation in the game and were unable to exert the dominance that Rodgers so badly desired and would allow them to find real stability.

The fixture schedule then threw up two very difficult away games, at Southampton and at Manchester United. While the Liverpool players were starting to gain a certain level of self-confidence, they still hadn't achieved that fluency which would allow them to arrive at any ground, impose their will and leave with all three points. These weren't games to try and frantically unleash their four forwards and rely too much on luck.

Brendan Rodgers therefore decided not to start with Raheem Sterling at St Mary's and to return to a midfield three with Gerrard, Henderson, and Joe Allen. Slightly fortuitously, Luis Suárez scored the first goal after sixteen minutes and then Liverpool showed the know-how they didn't have in December to handle a lead at a difficult ground. The team showed the increasing maturity it had been acquiring and that always essential evolution.

This would become even more evident a few minutes after the second half had started. Such a tight lead offered no guarantee of taking all three points, and Brendan Rodgers decided it was time to make an astute change. He decided to put Sterling on for Coutinho, but not as the simple change of a different player to occupy the same position, but as a tactical surprise to change things around for the opposition and exploit the spaces Southampton was leaving in its search for an equalizer.

In just a minute, Sterling went through the Saints' central line and fired in a Luis Suárez ball unopposed inside the area. It was a magical move by Brendan Rodgers because he didn't put him on the wing, as he normally did, but tried to change the pattern set by the opposition and offered something completely different and unexpected. Coutinho's precise distribution had now been replaced by Sterling's blistering pace, a change which caught Southampton completely off guard. Steven Gerrard applied the coup de grace near the end of the game, and Liverpool ended up putting down a real marker, which sent player motivation levels through the roof and reaffirmed them as proper Premier League title candidates.

The next week against David Moyes' erratic Manchester United side, the approach was the same. While the opponents didn't have the same solidity as Southampton, a visit to Old Trafford always meant a tense afternoon. Brendan Rodgers kept the three midfielders, but this time it was Coutinho who was left on the bench while Sterling started.

Liverpool cunningly waited for the fruit to fall from the tree under its own weight. Their great rivals weren't enjoying their best moment and that was something to be exploited in a very cool and calculated manner. It made more sense to go for a victory by a unanimous points decision at the end of the agreed number of rounds than try and win by a knockout at the start.

Manchester United made two clumsy mistakes which were both punished by Gerrard from the penalty spot. Another goal by Suárez near the end rewarded a Liverpool side who now seemed to have acquired the flexibility needed to know how to play depending on the opposition, the ground, and the situation in the game. They had shown that they were able to pounce on Arsenal and put four goals past them in twenty minutes, dominate possession, exert stifling pressure high up, and also be cautious enough and wait for the right moment to sink the knife into an eager but incoherent Manchester United side.

Brendan Rodgers very wisely decided to strengthen the team in stages. His first development phase was to attack better, unlike the approach other managers had and have adopted to get their teams out of a bad run. It's easier to find managers who decide to make their defense and midfield more robust in order to make them less vulnerable and more sure of themselves, and once they've managed that, then they start gradually freeing their formations to attack more until they get the balance they're looking for.

But Rodgers decided to start at the other end and showed that his theory also held water. The defense continued to be cavalier, and Liverpool struggled to keep a clean sheet, but their goal-scoring record meant that teams started playing less openly against them and to a certain point they managed to perform better defensively as a result of their scorching attack. It was exactly the opposite of what was happening at that time with Manchester United, who were respected less after Sir Alex Ferguson's departure because opponents knew that the Red Devils had faded to a pale pink.

Rodgers also had the good fortune that his different midfield options, whether with three men or two, had worked much better than he'd perhaps imagined, as obviously this area of the pitch isn't included in "attacking better." They were the same players as the season before, without any additions, so the change in performance levels was due solely to the cohesion achieved between them and the holistic evolution of the side.

But in the same way that such a drastic change could take place from one season to the next, an equivalent step backward could be experienced in just a few weeks, or much worse, from one game to the next. Liverpool's margin for error for winning the league was smaller than just one game, and Brendan Rodgers needed to be ready to avoid it. Indeed, changes for the worse are more common and more sudden than changes for good. The Liverpool midfield was still not as solid as the one the Kop had proclaimed as the best ever to anyone who would listen when they had Javier Mascherano, Xabi Alonso, and Steven Gerrard there. The patch needed to be ready before the hole appeared.

The games went by, and Liverpool was gathering three points every time they played, though not without the odd scare, like at West Ham United, a side who set up to offer a similar challenge to the one they had experienced against Aston Villa and Southampton. This was a game where it didn't appear so advisable to leave the midfield so unprotected and potentially unconnected to the four forwards given the back-to-basics, hard-tackling nature of the approach offered by Sam Allardyce.

However, Rodgers didn't realize this and played his four quick forwards at Upton Park as if he wanted to make the most of the impetus he had built up with them, forgetting how flexible he needed to be and what he should have learned in situations like this.

That day, Liverpool played one of their worst games of the season, especially in attack, where they were stifled by Big Sam's impenetrable web and where having four clearly defined attackers was of little use to them. After half-time, with the score at 1-1, Rodgers had to make the change of Lucas for Coutinho, again to revive his midfield and adopt a position that would allow him to win the game.

If luck was on Liverpool's side on any day that year, it was then. Another very controversial penalty gave the great skipper the chance to leave Liverpool's fate in their own hands with just five matches remaining.

As luck would have it, the fixture schedule saved the best excitement for the finishing straight, and in two of those five games Liverpool's caliber would really be put to the test. It was the reverse of the December fixtures against Manchester City and Chelsea, the chance to get revenge, but also to show how much Brendan Rodgers and his players had learned from those two defeats and from the roller-coaster ride they'd experienced up to April. The great defining month had arrived, and the denouement was like a knockout round in the Champions League, where what you had achieved quantitatively up to that point counted for little. It was almost a case of starting from zero again. A short league lasting 450 minutes.

City was Liverpool's main rival for the league while Chelsea had already dropped out of the battle after continuing to drop points against lower-ranked opposition. However, because of the way both teams played and what was at stake for one team but not the other, it was more likely that Liverpool would drop points against José Mourinho's team than Manuel Pellegrini's.

Against City, the four forwards started again, and in that game, it was entirely understandable that Brendan Rodgers should opt for that formation, as he had to ensure that the emotional factor was always on his side. Representing a latent threat from the first minute was going to be more intimidating than exercising a cold and calculating caution because as the minutes went by without the score line changing, Manchester

City would feel more at home. To allow that to happen would have been disastrous and something they may not have been able to recover from bearing in mind that Liverpool's main weapon, the one which fed their success and which had made it possible for them to win nine games in a row, was none other than the passionate grit and determination that had taken hold of their players.

Liverpool had a dream start to the game with a goal after six minutes and another one before the half-hour mark. This was just what Brendan Rodgers had been looking for with that lineup, but Manchester City was a long way from giving up, and the 2-0 score line was misleading for both teams. In the second half Liverpool began to feel the weakness of that approach as City started to dominate possession and play elaborately, and the Liverpool forwards were running around after the ball like headless chickens.

While in other similar situations putting a midfielder on in place of an attacker helped give balance to the team without affecting their attacking capabilities too much, to do so now would have been seen as a clearly defensive move and would have sent a direct message to Manchester City. This Liverpool side didn't have the audacity of Barça, Bayern, or the German national team to dominate such a tense game against such a hard opponent and in such an extreme situation just by virtue of playing with three men in midfield. Above all else, Brendan Rodgers couldn't afford for Liverpool to relinquish the emotional control of the game, even though the opposition was threatening to take it from them.

Rodgers felt that putting Joe Allen or Lucas on, despite the different dynamic they would stamp on the match, would have been like taking a perhaps irreversible step backward. He had to continue to cling to abandon and let freedom rather than confinement be what decided this unique situation. There was to be no looking back. He had to keep going forward with the same momentum to the bitter end. All or nothing!

But Sturridge's injury four minutes after City had drawn level left him with no other option, and he was forced to put Joe Allen on. Liverpool defused the City attack, but they were unable to impose a rhythm which might guarantee the third goal and that essential victory, much less find the breakneck speed of the first half again. It was another mistake by Kompany, who had a hand in all three Liverpool goals, that paved the way to victory.

The built-up adrenaline exploded at Mark Clattenburg's full-time whistle and reached its crescendo with Steven Gerrard's legendary tirade in the middle of the pitch, where he exhorted his colleagues to forget that game and go and do exactly the same at Norwich. The great captain said straight after the game that those had been the longest ninety minutes of his career, but it was perhaps also the game with the biggest range of emotions and where the team's heart was more important than all its purely footballing artillery.

That same surge of emotion led Jordan Henderson to make an ugly challenge in the final minutes which cost him a red card and a three-game suspension. Liverpool would face the key away games at Norwich and Crystal Palace without him, as well as the home game against Chelsea, where they would perhaps need his presence most.

Despite having already dropped out of the title race, Mourinho wasn't going to gift Liverpool the sweet taste of glory. In practice, that game was of no importance to him, but it's not his style to let others achieve any kind of success at his cost. In a way he was being fair, because Chelsea had turned up for both Manchester City games and had taken all six points.

Brendan Rodgers was forced to start with Gerrard, Allen, and Lucas in midfield. Sturridge was only just back from injury against Manchester

City and wasn't ready to start, but if he'd been available Rodgers would almost certainly have started with his four regular forwards.

In the first half, although Liverpool didn't score, they matched an opponent who had more of a defensive nastiness and whose primary objective was to provoke mistakes in the opposition in order to strike a blow. With several players starting who weren't regulars, it was almost impossible for Chelsea to take on a more proactive role.

When they went behind from the completely abnormal situation of Gerrard's slip, Liverpool just went in search of a win with their attacking zeal as a weapon, but they still had the same cold and calculating team in front of them, and that team now felt even more comfortable on a very familiar ground, a goal up and feeling their opponent's frustration up close. The second goal was simply a consequence of this, and the unbeaten run Liverpool had started in December after losing to Chelsea was ended by the same opponent because of the same inability to destroy their web.

The absence of Henderson and Sturridge's lack of match fitness was impossible to make up for with the rest of the players available because Brendan Rodgers had kept to a small nucleus of players thanks to the lack of European competitions. The starters didn't need to be rotated too much because they basically played every weekend, so when two key players were missing in a critical game, there were few answers to be found because those questions hadn't been asked since August.

The dream of the title was smashed to pieces on that fateful Monday night at Crystal Palace when they threw away a three-goal lead in just ten minutes. While the revolution offered by Brendan Rodgers bore its fruit from January to April, the harvest wasn't big enough to overcome all the challenges the season presented before him.

The summer brought the sale of Suárez, Sturridge's endless injuries, and the arrival of a large handful of new players, collapsing everything Rodgers had built in the preceding months because it never became something genuinely solid, but had indirectly benefited from the good fortune that the players clicked together and from the extent to which football relies on luck.

Chapter 9

SUFFERING—THE ROAD TO GLORY AND MAKING DECISIONS IN FOOTBALL

In life, any process that leads to some type of success will be implicitly full of suffering. However great that glory may be, the body and the mind end up saying "enough" for a period of time or forever.

Sport, and more specifically football, is perhaps one of the examples that best illustrates the cost of achieving something that might be considered success. This is not winning a league, or two, or even a Champions League. Besides winning a certain number of trophies, it's retaining a coherence in all aspects surrounding football club management for a considerable period.

Success can not only be considered in the big clubs. In the medium-sized and small clubs, by performing a logical correlation of the potential objectives, it can also be achieved, even if it doesn't find its expression in the lifting of any trophies. For the big institutions, the most common and latent gauge is obviously the trophies won, and it's very difficult to increase this collection if there are areas of the organization which aren't functioning correctly.

There is the example of one club that had uninterrupted success for twenty years, which translated into all kinds of trophies, the extensive use of youth academy players, and the time players and manager stayed on the books and had sustained performance levels from the team. Obviously, this is none other than Manchester United.

It was always to be expected that after the departure of the man who led them for so long, the team would go through a difficult period. It's like when you take a stitch out and the skin doesn't heal immediately, you have to wait a while for it to recover completely because the suture had stuck so much to the organism that it practically formed a part of it.

Perhaps the key to this sustained success was that in all the world Sir Alex Ferguson is the manager who best understands the suffering that goes with maintaining that level and how essential it is to play with that suffering in order for your rhythm to not be affected. In principle, it might be thought that the Manchester United squads that he managed were quite large, so too much playing time had to be shared between players who might have been regular starters at other clubs. However, although we might think rotation is unfair, if we look at the bigger picture we can see that it was the key to Manchester United being able to maintain the same high level for so long.

In moving his pieces around like that, Ferguson avoided all his players suffering at the same time, and he reserved part of his squad so that he could use them when the men who had played most in the most recent mini-cycle had reached a pathological accumulation of suffering. Ferguson broke his team into inner cycles where there were fixed starters (Rooney, Vidić, Ferdinand, Evra, Ronaldo) and players who had specific roles, whom he kept back so they could play an important part after the cycle change.

Indeed, within the same season, and this was seen much more in the side's successful seasons, Ferguson rarely used the same starting eleven in two matches running. In the 2008-2009 season—when they won the Premier League for the third year in a row, reached the Champions League final, played in and won the World Club Championship, won the League Cup, and reached the FA Cup semi-final—such a good return wouldn't have been possible without a very judicious rotation by the manager.

Ferguson himself said so in public on several occasions: the miles run and travelled, the matches with their national teams, and, although he didn't say it, the suffering, all made rotation necessary. He was the only one who was able to master this art to perfection and ensure that the team's level didn't drop.

That's the difference between him and so many others who wanted to do the same thing but never managed it. Under his management, Manchester United was the only team in the world elite where the vast majority of the players who played less never felt like reserves, but felt like they were strategic cogs in the team wheel that needed them in order to keep turning to the end.

Football is perhaps one of the sciences where decision-making acquires a vital meaning. What the directors and managers decide invariably influences the fate of their clubs, just as the steps taken by the players shape the direction their careers take. Nowadays, decisions are increasingly made for monetary reasons, as football is moving further and further away from its purely sporting core and is becoming instead a ruthless source of business, investment, and wealth, although not everyone has managed to take advantage of it.

We can find countless examples of players who have destroyed their careers because they weren't able to make the wisest decisions. Michael

Owen went to a Real Madrid side that was full of star forwards. Kaká went to the same team knowing that Cristiano Ronaldo was just about to be signed. David Bentley left Blackburn Rovers and went to Tottenham Hotspur to compete with Aaron Lennon for a place. Alexandre Song left Arsenal to play for Barça. Radamel Falcao followed the money bubble to Monaco, and when he saw that the project he'd been promised wouldn't materialize, he went to Manchester United and Chelsea on loan where the competition for places would be fierce. The list is, frankly, endless. On the other hand, one of the most sensible and well-made decisions in recent years was Jamie Vardy's when he decided not to go to Arsenal and to stay at Leicester City, a side whose approach suits his playing style better and which, at the age of twenty-nine, he saw as a safer option for his future.

A case that illustrates well how much a bad signing can cost both the club that signs him and the player himself was Andriy Shevchenko joining Chelsea. When he still had all his goal-scoring faculties, Shevchenko decided to leave AC Milan and follow Roman Abramovich's checkbook, perhaps without looking too closely into the characteristics of his new team. Being a regular starter at Chelsea was synonymous with competing with Didier Drogba, because it wasn't completely clear beforehand that Mourinho was going to try and play with them both up front. Add to this the fact that a change of club, country, and lifestyle always causes great uncertainty and the fact that a series of factors can affect a player's performance. Moving away from your comfort zone is always going to have a greater or lesser psychological effect. Thinking of yourself as a superstar isn't always the only thing to bear in mind when it comes to exploring new horizons.

The signing of Shevchenko by Chelsea killed his career, and he became one of the worst footballing investments of all time. Two years were completely wasted, making him lose form and marking the start of the end of a brilliant career when he was still at the peak of his powers.

Another example is what happened to Radamel Falcao when he wanted to escape from Monaco after his first season. He chose Manchester United first, and then Chelsea, teams where there was much more competition than he was fit enough to face so soon after recovering from ligament damage. He was going to war without any weapons.

But when he returned to Monaco in 2016, he found a completely different landscape; now he was a first-team regular, captain, and reference point for the team's attack. He no longer had to compete with anyone, he felt secure, fulfilled, focused. He recovered his lethal finishing prowess, became a Ligue 1 winner, and reached the Champions League semi-final.

That's why a player must know about the inner workings of the team he's thinking of going to, know the manager, how he thinks, the players in the squad, assess the chances he has to play and in what position, and have enough self-awareness to have an idea of how he's going to react to the change.

Every player must study transfers as if they were job offers. At the end of the day, however much we try to see football from a non-commercial perspective, for them it's their job. You can't blindly accept a place only going on the salary offered. Sometimes when you earn less money you earn more in other aspects, like getting continuity on the pitch, not having to compete unnecessarily with other players for a place in the starting lineup, and reducing the effect of those psychological and environmental factors that have a decisive impact on a player's career.

There are some players who perform better without the pressure of competing for a place, while others find that when they feel a little competition it helps them to not let their form drop. It all comes down to what motivates different individuals.

A manager must also know a player's personality before he signs him, and he must be fairly sure that he will continue to be motivated in his new team, that he will adapt quickly, and that his form won't drop, particularly in the positions where audacity and impudence are needed. When they get to a new club many players become so inhibited that they don't exploit their potential because they've lost the leadership they enjoyed at their previous clubs.

When a player is his team's reference point, and he goes to a different club where there's already a well-established order, he's very likely to find it difficult to keep playing at the same level because part of his footballing potential consisted of that leadership role. The greater the caliber of his new club, the more difficult it will be for him. This happens less in defensive positions, where players generally adapt more quickly and their levels of performance don't drop, although the arrival of Walter Samuel and Fabio Cannavaro at Real Madrid might be considered two of the exceptions to the rule.

The PSV Eindhoven Mark van Bommel, captain, box-to-box midfielder, free kick- and penalty-taker, and team leader on the pitch, was never the same either at Barça or at Bayern. In both clubs he came across too many established players, and he was far from being their footballing reference point.

Many clubs sign a player based solely on his performance in one single season, and in many cases they don't get the expected results. Generally, hasty decisions do not lead to stability. There are players who turn out to be one-season wonders, but to be sure of the quality of what is being bought you need a coherent amount of evidence.

A case that illustrates this idea to perfection was Robinho's decision to go to Manchester City and not Chelsea when he was forced out of Real Madrid. In the summer of 2007, in the period of transition between

Fabio Capello and Bernd Schuster, the then-president Ramón Calderón managed to complete one of his great dream signings, Arjen Robben. This was something of an indulgence, because Robinho was already playing on the left wing; he had fit in perfectly in that position and was undoubtedly one of the best players in the side.

But that didn't matter. Robben came and sparked tension in the dressing room together with positional changes. When they both started, one of the two had to change wing, and at the end of the season, having seen that Schuster preferred Robben, Robinho got fed up and pressed for a move.

Chelsea, the very club Robben had moved from and which had the backing of Abramovich's disproportionate checkbook, put a tempting offer on the table. But Manchester City's new owners had a very similar modus operandi to the Russian magnate and were also forthright in their intention of getting Robinho.

The Brazilian player was sensible when he came to analyze both proposals—and perhaps many others which were presented to him—and chose City, a club on a financial upswing that had had a reasonably acceptable season with Sven Göran Eriksson.

Here Robinho would be the king in his position. He wouldn't have to fight for a place with all the megastars Chelsea had on their books, and he would be able to continue to be a regular in the Brazilian national side. Although the team's results didn't meet expectations and Mark Hughes' work was far from being considered acceptable, Robinho had a good season and kept his international reputation intact.

The 2016 European Championship coincided with one of the fiercest transfer markets in recent years. Manchester United, Manchester City, and Chelsea had had a mediocre year and with the arrival of their new managers they set about ruthlessly restructuring their squads. It wasn't just them; other big teams in the top European leagues were working tirelessly in the busiest months for agents.

The managers of the national teams involved in a World Cup or a European Championship don't normally allow players to negotiate their transfers during the competition so they aren't distracted from their primary focus. However, this is practically impossible to fully enforce.

Radja Nainggolan, the excellent Roma midfielder, said hours before the European Championship started that Antonio Conte—who after finishing his duties as Italy manager at the tournament would become the new Chelsea manager—had tried to sign him when he was at Juventus and now he was putting pressure on him to go to Stamford Bridge.

> *"Conte told me what he expects from me and what type of player I can be for him. I'll never be a player who'll score 20 goals or give 20 assists, I'm not the one who'll be in the picture all the time. I can be important for a team. A manager who appreciates that is important for me,"* said Nainggolan.

But deep down he wasn't sure if it was worth leaving Italy after twelve years. If he finally decided to do so he didn't want a small improvement, but an abrupt change in his career. "*You could say: 'Why not try it in England?' But you can ask the question the other way too: 'Why would I leave everything behind to fail over there?*'" Nainggolan wondered.[44]

In the end, the Belgian decided to stay at Roma for now, and although he'll not earn as much there as he would at Chelsea, he simply felt that it wasn't worth risking his career just at the time when he was at the top of his form. His freedom, his influence on the pitch, and the stability he's achieved in his life are worth more than an adventure that might bear fruit, but for which there are so many other examples where the experience ended up being disastrous, just like Shevchenko.

This decision may change soon, and if communication between him and Conte continues to be so good then he may make the move as a carefully thought out decision and not because of mere financial interest. The risk of failure is always latent, and it can never be eliminated completely, however psychologically strong you are or however ideal the conditions may seem in the destination you chose. In football, there are too many variables, and it's impossible to keep them all under control, even for a Ronaldo, a Messi or a Zlatan. It's all down to personal preference and what each individual judges to be best for their career.

Speaking of Roma and decisions which change your life, there may be no better example of how professional success doesn't depend on the amount of money you earn or the number of trophies you win.

Francesco Totti tells in the very interesting *The Players' Tribune* blog of how when he was thirteen there was a knock on the door of the apartment where he lived with his parents. His mother went to open it and found a group of men who said they were football directors. But they weren't from Roma, the team Totti had in his blood and where his great idol, Giuseppe Giannini, played. Those men were representatives of AC Milan, the European Cup champions at that time.

Fiorella, his mother, and his boss according to Totti, decided for him. "*Mi dispiace. No, no*," was the answer she gave the men in red and black, completely sure of what she was doing. "*My mother taught me a lesson that day: 'Your home is the most important thing in life*,'" Francesco explained.[45]

In this case Rome was the city where Totti was born, had grown up, and where he could have a brilliant future as a professional and a person;

nothing could be closer to the definition of *home* in the truest sense of the word. For other players *home* may be the team where they have cemented their career, the city where they have made their lives, or the environment that injects them with confidence, fulfilment, and life.

Unfortunately, football today is pulled along by less human interests, which stop us from seeing more Francesco Totti's and where *home* has in most cases become the place where the most money can be earned. Happiness has changed the parameters which define it and because of that we see how, for example, Mario Götze and Robert Lewandowski changed Borussia Dortmund for their biggest rivals, Bayern Munich, to finally put an end to the last remaining vestige of competitiveness in the Bundesliga. For Götze, in particular, the move wasn't a happy one, as after three disastrous seasons he tried to rescue his career by seeking refuge back in the team he had left after Bayern activated his release clause.

Another of the consequences of post-modern football and its dependent relationship with income is the urgency of success. Many of the magnates who have taken ownership of clubs in recent years want their capital to multiply immediately, but aren't aware that a good football team isn't built overnight, however many top stars fill the dressing room and even if one of the best managers in the world is brought in. This would be an expensive football team anyway. That's why it's now so difficult to see a product of the youth academy find a place in the first team at Manchester City, Chelsea, Liverpool, or even Manchester United.

Now, for the vast majority of clubs it's even more difficult to maintain a stable squad given the continual departures of players and managers. There's not much doubt about it; if you don't perform immediately, you never earn yourself a place. If you get injured, even though you may have been your manager's favorite at one time, you can lose your place for good. What happened with Francesco Totti at Roma is like something from a different world these days, as is a cycle like Sir Alex Ferguson's at Manchester United or Arsène Wenger's at Arsenal.

Unfortunately, it's the managers who almost always get the blame when they don't achieve instant success. A case in point from the recent past is Carlo Ancelotti at Real Madrid, sacked after not winning anything in his second season, even though he won the Champions League and the Copa del Rey in his first.

Ancelotti told the German newspaper *Die Welt* at the beginning of September 2016 that the reason for his departure was the obsession at the Bernabéu with winning trophies. "*We reached the Champions League semi-finals and missed out by a point on winning La Liga. At Real Madrid, stability means that you must win. Always. That was it for me*," the Italian said.[46]

Florentino Pérez couldn't bear the fact that Ancelotti didn't win the Spanish league in either of his two seasons in charge, and that to make matters worse, Barça should win a treble. But then what should we make of the decision he took? He replaced Ancelotti with Rafa Benítez, a man who had won his last league title eleven years earlier with Valencia, despite having managed at well-established clubs like Liverpool and Inter. With all due respect, you need to think ten times before you sack Ancelotti and bring in Benítez.

For smaller clubs it's more and more difficult to hold on to their best players because the financial disparity with the richer clubs ends up taking them away. Success has become so ephemeral and so impossible to stretch over time that it's sometimes understandable that managers want to leave after winning a trophy, or even without having won one.

Ancelotti found a completely different outlook when he got to Bayern Munich. Although it's a European giant on a par with Real Madrid, the club is managed by ex-players, rather than businessmen, who know how difficult it is to win trophies even when you're the strongest team in the league. This footballing and commercial income-generating machine couldn't get to the Champions League final in three years with one of the best managers in the world in Pep Guardiola.

Although he doesn't consider the practice of beheading managers when they don't get instant success a fair one, Carlo Ancelotti accepts the outlook with a certain feeling of resignation. "*I have to respect it. A club is not going to criticise itself or its players. They are the strength of the club*," he continued in his comments to *Die Welt*. He feels happy that Bayern is run more like a family and that there's not that external pressure to be champion of everything every season.

That's precisely the quality that post-modern football seems to be losing most quickly, the family quality, the quality where money isn't the most important thing or the *raison d'*être. If from the start of modern football around thirty years ago to today's post-modern version the changes have been huge, football in a thousand years' time—if football still exists then, and assuming that it will cease to exist when the world does—will not resemble the current version very much.

Just as a good team can't be built overnight, the decisions which may bring football closer to its truest essence again won't bear fruit in just a few years. Unfortunately, the time needed to return purity to a system or an institution is much greater than the time needed for its degeneration. The direction in football today is heading and many of the decisions that influence it are only serving to polarize it more and more and leaving the opportunity to win trophies open to a small few—those whose owners place them in a kingship which it's possible to leave, but which you can only join if you're backed by a benefactor's checkbook.

It is, therefore, the true football men who have to smooth the road and allow football to belong exclusively to the fans and the players again, as it is they who are ultimately the only agents who are really important in this story, and the ones who see it as such. Now is the time to take far-reaching decisions to humanize the game and stop, for example, N'Golo Kanté from joining Chelsea after the fantastic season he had with Leicester City, with whom he won perhaps the most exciting league title of his career.

But modern society doesn't seem able to appreciate that paradigm of happiness, the one which always seemed irreplaceable to Francesco Totti and because of which he is one of the biggest legends in this football we have to live with now, even though he has only ever won one Scudetto with Roma and has never been crowned champion of Europe, and his bank account isn't as swollen as that of Cristiano Ronaldo or Zlatan Ibrahimović.

At the end of the day, to reach the summit, as Claudio Ranieri said in his piece on *The Players' Tribune*, you don't need a big name or a big contract; instead "*You just need to keep an open mind, an open heart, a full battery, and run free*."[47]

This is the time to set to work to see Deportivo La Coruña crowned champions of Spain again, Borussia Mönchengladbach the *Meister* of the Bundesliga, Everton win the Premier League, and Ajax rule Europe again. It is possible. Football and the world need it.

REFERENCES

1 Carlo Ancelotti. 2016. France and Portugal must remember that the key thing in preparing for a tournament final is simplicity. *The Telegraph*.

2 Cristiano Ronaldo. 2009. Quoted in Cristiano Ronaldo blames tactics for Rome defeat. *The Telegraph*.

3 César Luis Menotti. 2009. Quoted in *Com Ràdio* interview.

4 Carlo Ancelotti. 2009. Quoted in Il mio calcio Libero Ancelotti a cuore aperto E non dite che sono buono. *La Repubblica*.

5 Carlo Ancelotti. 2016. Quoted in Ancelotti: Zidane changed the way I saw football. *Goal*.

6 Sir Alex Ferguson. 2016. Quoted in Champions League Technical Topics. Season 2015-2016. *UEFA.com*.

7 Arsène Wenger. 2016. Quoted from Arsenal versus Manchester City post-match press conference.

8 Arsène Wenger. 2015. Quoted from Arsenal versus Aston Villa pre-match press conference. *Sky Sports*.

9 Lionel Messi. 2016. Quoted from Arsenal versus FC Barcelona post-match press conference. *TV3*.

10 Arsène Wenger. 2016. Quoted from Everton versus Arsenal post-match press conference.

11 Arsène Wenger. 2017. Quoted in *BT Sport* interview.

12 Arsenal Supporters' Trust. 2013. From *AST Survey results 2013 - Fans back Wenger but want transfer and wage bill changes*.

13 Arsenal Supporters' Trust. 2013. From *Arsène Wenger has much to do to earn a new contract at Arsenal*.

14 Arsenal Supporters' Trust. 2015. Statement from *Supporters Forum*.

15 Arsenal Supporters' Trust. 2017. From *AST Survey*.

16 Roberto Mancini. 2011. Quoted from Manchester City versus West Bromwich Albion pre-match press conference.

17 Sir Alex Ferguson. 2015. *Leading*. Hachette Book Group.

18 Manuel Pellegrini. 2015. Quoted from Manchester City versus FC Barcelona post-match press conference.

19 Manuel Pellegrini. 2016. Quoted in If I don't get an interesting offer I will quit football. *The Guardian*.

20 Josep Guardiola. 2016. Quoted from press conference in China.

21 Josep Guardiola. 2016. Quoted from Manchester City versus Southampton post-match press conference.

22 Sir Alex Ferguson. 2015. *Leading*. Hachette Book Group.

23 Josep Guardiola. 2014. *Herr Pep*. Roca Editorial.

24 Josep Guardiola. 2017. Quoted from Monaco versus Manchester City post-match press conference.

25 Josep Guardiola. 2014. *Herr Pep*. Roca Editorial.

26 Barcelona lost the first leg of the European Cup semi-final against Gothenburg in 1986 3-0. But they managed to win the second leg by the same score line, forced the game into penalties, and won in the shootout.

27 Theo Walcott. 2010. Quoted from Arsenal versus FC Barcelona post-match press conference.

28 Josep Guardiola. 2011. Quoted from Real Sociedad versus FC Barcelona post-match press conference.

29 José Mourinho. 2010. Quoted from FC Barcelona versus Real Madrid post-match press conference.

30 José Mourinho. 2010. Quoted from Real Madrid versus Valencia post-match press conference.

31 José Mourinho. 2007. Quoted in *Mourinho, ¿por qué tantas victorias?* by Bruno Oliveira, Nuno Resende, Nuno Amierio, and Ricardo Barreto. MC Sports.

32 José Mourinho. 2012. Quoted from Sevilla versus Real Madrid post-match press conference.

33 José Mourinho. 2010. Quoted in *José Mourinho, Special Leadership* by Luis Lourenço. Prime Books.

34 José Mourinho. 2013. Quoted from Chelsea versus Basel pre-match press conference.

35 José Mourinho. 2013. Quoted from Chelsea versus Basel post-match press conference.

36 Jamie Redknapp. 2013. Jose Mourinho must find best Chelsea system. *Sky Sports*.

37 José Mourinho. 2013. Quoted from Chelsea versus Fulham pre-match press conference.

38 José Mourinho. 2013. Quoted from Chelsea versus Fulham post-match press conference.

39 José Mourinho. 2013. Quoted from Sunderland versus Chelsea post-match press conference.

40 José Mourinho. 2013. Quoted from Arsenal versus Chelsea post-match press conference.

41 Louis van Gaal. 2016. Quoted from Manchester United versus Bournemouth pre-match press conference.

42 Robin van Persie. 2015. Quoted in *The Sunday Times*.

43 David Gill. 2015. Quoted in Former Man Utd chief executive David Gill lifts the lid on Sir Alex, the Glazers, Sepp Blatter, Moyes and his favourite ever signing. *Manchester Evening News*.

44 Radja Nainggolan. 2016. Quoted from European Championship 2016 pre-tournament press conference.

45 Francesco Totti. 2016. Per Roma. *The Players' Tribune*.

46 Carlo Ancelotti. 2016. Quoted in Eine Herzens-Wut kann ich nicht kontrollieren. *Die Welt*.

47 Claudio Ranieri. 2016. Quoted in We do not dream. *The Players' Tribune*.

CREDITS

DESIGN AND LAYOUT

Cover Design: Katerina Georgieva

Interior Design and Layout: Astrid Stähr

EDITING

Translator: James Peel

Editor: Richard Sheehan

Managing Editor: Elizabeth Evans

Subscribe to our newsletter at **www.m-m-sports.com**

MORE GREAT SOCCER TITLES

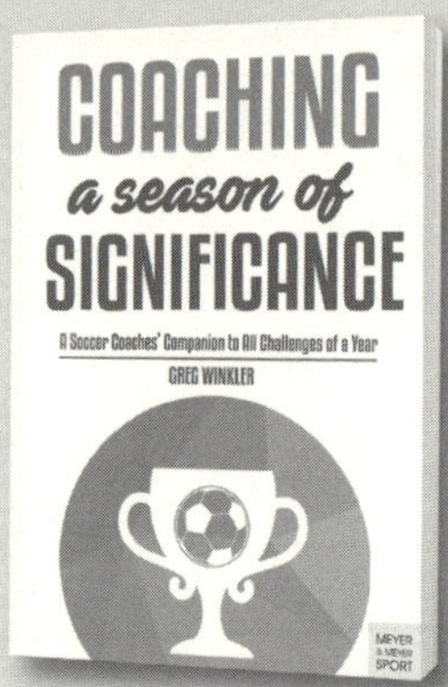

1st edition
160 p., b/w, paperback,
2 illustrations
5.5" x 8.5"
ISBN: 9781782551065
$9.95 US

Greg Winkler

COACHING A SEASON OF SIGNIFICANCE

A Soccer Coaches' Companion to All Challenges of a Year

Coaches are always looking for tools and resources to improve their craft, from training programs to team management. *Coaching a Season of Significance* was written by an experienced youth and high school soccer coach for other soccer coaches. However, many of the thoughts and ideas can be transferred and utilized in other forms of sport and in business.

This book takes you from the beginning to the end of the season, explaining how to implement core values for your program, build strong communication, and foster long-lasting relationships. Along with team rules, dealing with administration, and program promotion, this comprehensive guide covers many topics concerning soccer and coaching in general.

FROM MEYER & MEYER SPORT

168 p., b/w, paperback
8 illustrations
5.5" x 8.5"
ISBN: 9781782550280
$14.95 US

Shane Stay

WHY AMERICAN SOCCER ISN'T THERE YET

Why American Soccer Isn't There Yet analyzes the methods of Brazil, Spain, Holland–where the author has lived and played–and other similar nations, establishing a new vision for the approach to American soccer. The purpose is to establish a new insight into contemporary American soccer and show it has the potential to become a prominent world power. The majority of American soccer players have athletic talent, the raw physical ability, and often the technical ability, but they have been fed the wrong mental information from their coaches and family. This book identifies the core problem and how to fix it for the future of American soccer.

MEYER & MEYER Sport
Von-Coels-Str. 390
52080 Aachen
Germany

Phone	+49 02 41 - 9 58 10 - 13
Fax	+49 02 41 - 9 58 10 - 10
E-Mail	sales@m-m-sports.com
E-Books	www.m-m-sports.com

All books available as E-books.

MEYER & MEYER SPORT